PRIVATE LIMITED COMPANIES:
Formation and Management

PRIVATE LIMITED COMPANIES:
Formation and Management

by

Gordon H. Brough, LL.B. (Hons), Dip. L.P.,
Solicitor

W. GREEN/Sweet & Maxwell
EDINBURGH
1997

First published 1990
Second edition 1997

ISBN 0 414 01224 0

No natural forests were destroyed to make this product;
only farmed timber was used and replanted

A CIP catalogue reference for this book is available from the British Library

Typeset by Trinity Typesetting, Edinburgh
Printed in Great Britain by Redwood Books, Wiltshire

ACKNOWLEDGEMENTS

In preparing this second edition I have, as always, received considerable assistance from the lawyers and support staff at my firm. Mr Robert Edwards of Arthur Andersen has again kept me right on taxation matters. I would like to record my gratitude to all those concerned. I would also like to thank my wife, Linda, and our children, Fraser and Clarice, for their forbearance and support.

CONTENTS

CHAPTER 1

INTRODUCTION

The aim of this book is a modest one. It seeks to provide an introduction to company law and to deal, in particular, with the formation and management of private limited companies. As a result, little or no reference has been made to the taxation of limited companies nor to the substantial body of law dealing with the appointment of receivers, administrators and liquidators.

The text is based upon a series of tutorials and lectures on company law addressed to university students about to enter into practice as solicitors. As such, the text is intended to be practically based rather than academic in nature. A deliberate attempt has been made to minimise the reference to case law and instead to concentrate on the statutory provisions and their application in practice. Further to the practical aim of the work, a number of precedents have been provided in the various Schedules. It is hoped that these will not be followed slavishly but will give a flavour of the type of document which might be adopted.

Company law is becoming increasingly complicated and in all but the most simple cases, legal and accounting advice will be required by those wishing to set up companies or to alter the structure of existing companies or to do anything outwith the ordinary day-to-day trading of the company. Much of the legislation in this area in the last two decades has been influenced or even dictated by the directives of the European Community. A work of this nature cannot do more than touch upon this vast area of development. A summary of the present European directives relating to company law and those proposed is, however, included within Schedule 1. Information on the European influence in relation to company law and on any particular point can also be sought from the Department of Trade and Industry at 1–19 Victoria Street, London SW1 or by telephone on 01179 444 888.

CHAPTER 2

REASONS FOR INCORPORATION

The Company's Legal Persona

2.1 The success of the limited company as a legal device and, more importantly, as a business medium, flows directly from the law's acceptance that for almost all purposes the company is to be viewed as a legal entity separate and distinct from its members who own it and its directors who manage it. It has its own rights and liabilities which are divorced, in the main, from those of the individuals who are involved with it. This legal fiction which separates the company from its members is generally referred to as the corporate veil. This position was established in the case *Salomon v. A. Salomon & Co. Ltd* [1897] A.C. 22. Aron Salomon may not be remembered for the boots and shoes that were his trade but he has left his mark upon company law and provided every writer on the subject with a useful starting point. The facts are worth recounting.

Salomon, as stated, was in the shoe trade. His business thrived and in 1892 he formed a company in which he himself, his wife and his five children were shareholders. In fact his wife and children held only one share each. The company bought the business from Salomon for £39,000 paying for it by giving Salomon shares and debentures in the company itself. Accordingly Salomon became not only a member of the company, being the registered holder of most of the company's shares, but also a creditor of the company as the holder of secured debentures, a form of loan. Quickly, for reasons outwith his control, the business began to falter and finally the company went into liquidation. The liquidator wished the incorporation struck down and, drawing back the corporate veil, sought to have Salomon rendered liable for the company's debts. The court held to the contrary. The company had been properly incorporated and was a separate legal entity from Salomon himself. Not only was he not liable to the company's creditors for the debts of the business but he was entitled to recover the money due by the company to himself as the holder of secured debentures in preference to the trade creditors.

Crucial to this decision was the absence of any fraud on the part of Salomon. There are cases in which the courts will refuse to allow the members of a company to hide behind the company's legal identity — cases when the courts will "lift the corporate veil". Unfortunately there is no single general principle underlying these cases. Many arise from the requirements of the Inland Revenue or from the accounting regulations contained in the Companies Act 1985 as amended by the Companies Act 1989 (particularly with regard to groups of related companies). The remainder are principally intended to avoid fraud or outright deception on the part of those running a company. Particular examples are set out below.

In the case of a public company where the number of members falls below two under section 24 of the Companies Act 1985. After six months the remaining member may, if he is aware of the position, be liable for any debts incurred by the company if the following three criteria are all met: 2.1.1

(a) the person was a member of the company following the expiration of the six month period;
(b) the person knew that the company was carrying on business with only one member; and
(c) the debts were contracted during the period following the expiration of the six month period.

This provision formerly applied to all companies but since the introduction of single member private companies in 1992 now only applies to public companies.

Either fraudulent or wrongful trading by directors under Part IV, Chapter X of the Insolvency Act 1986 or trading under the name of a previously insolvent company in contravention of section 216 of that Act. These matters will be dealt with in detail in Chapter 6. 2.1.2

Where the company is misdescribed on cheques or other negotiable instruments under section 349 of the Companies Act 1985. A director who signs the cheque will be personally liable to the payee if the company fails to pay. By way of illustration, in *Hendon v. Adelman* (1973) 117 S.J. 63, the directors of L. & R. Agencies Limited purported to sign a cheque for the company by writing L. R. Agencies Limited. The directors were held personally liable because in omitting "&" from the name they had failed to use the company's correct name. It should be noted however that despite the foregoing example the use of "Ltd" instead of "Limited"; "PLC" instead of "Public Limited Company" and "Co." instead of "Company" is permissible and will not result in directors being made personally liable. As a general principle it is immaterial that the person relying on the cheque or whatever was not misled as to the correct name of the company but there is case law in England which indicates that if the defect is minor and the person seeking to 2.1.3

find the directors personally liable was not misled then the person may be personally barred from claiming against the directors. In Scotland however the general principle is more rigidly adhered to and the Scottish courts are considerably stricter with directors in this matter.

A point of interest to readers involved in the manufacturing, assembling or supply business is that while the failure to use the company's full name on business letters, cheques, promissory notes, official publications, etc. may result in the imposition of fines and, in terms of section 349 (4), personal liability on the directors involved, the company's name may be affixed to goods manufactured, assembled or supplied by the company (subject to there being no prohibition on affixation) in a contracted form since such goods do not fall within the terms of section 349 (1) of the Act. It is also common for companies to operate under a trade or business name which is often a contraction of their full company name and which is given on the company's notepaper, etc. This is likewise unobjectionable provided that the full name of the company is legibly printed elsewhere on the notepaper; usually at the foot of the page.

2.1.4 *Where a company is obliged to make up and register group accounts incorporating the affairs of its subsidiaries under Part VII and Schedules 4 and 4A of the Companies Act 1985.* There may be a number of companies which, while they are technically separate legal entities by virtue of the corporate veil are, in commercial reality, linked together as members of a group of companies in terms of section 227 of the Act. The company which is the parent undertaking is, unless exempted under sections 228, 229, 248 and 249 of the Act, required to prepare and lodge group accounts consolidating the figures from its subsidiary undertakings which are effectively viewed for that purpose not as separate entities but as "divisions" of the parent undertaking.

2.1.5 *In cases of fraud or improper conduct at common law.* In *Gilford Motor Company Ltd v. Horne* [1933] Ch. 935, for example, Horne set up a company to run a business in order to avoid a restrictive covenant in terms of his previous contract of employment whereby he had undertaken not to compete with his previous employers. His former employers, the Gilford Motor Company Limited, raised an action to restrain Horne from so operating. This action was successful, the court describing the company as "a mere cloak or sham" intended by Horne as a device for avoiding his obligations to his previous employers.

2.1.6 *For tax purposes.* Although the tax system follows general law in treating a company as a taxable person independent of its owners, the veil of incorporation is lifted in specific circumstances both to protect the taxpayer and the flow of funds to the Inland Revenue. An example of the former is the so-called "imputation system" whereby the tax which a company pays when it makes a dividend (Advance Corporation Tax) is "imputed" to the shareholder receiving the dividend. Thus the shareholder is regarded as having met his basic rate tax liability on the dividend income. On the other hand there are numerous anti-avoidance provisions, for example to tax parent companies on the profits of their subsidiaries located in tax havens, or to "apportion" for inheritance tax purposes dispositions by certain companies known as "close companies" (broadly, those with five or fewer participators). The effect of "apportionment" is to treat the participators as if they themselves have made the disposition. More sweeping Revenue powers to "apportion" the income of close companies to their participators were abolished in the 1989 Finance Act.

Where it is necessary to establish the residence of a company. For example 2.1.7
where it is necessary to establish whether or not a company is to be treated as an enemy alien or where the residence of a company is relevant for tax purposes. To ascertain the residence of a company the court will look behind the corporate veil and, looking beyond the place of registration, determine its residence by reference to the place of the company's central management and control. The courts will determine in what country the central management and control lies by looking at all the circumstances and generally decide on a "common sense" basis. For example the court may decide that the place of residence is, say, Germany because the board of directors is based there or because the autocratic managing director is based there. It should also be noted that it is possible for a company to be resident in more than one country at once although special provisions may apply for tax purposes, however the ability of a company incorporated in the United Kingdom to be "dually" resident was significantly reduced by the 1994 Finance Act.

The foregoing are examples only and by no means constitute an 2.1.8
exhaustive list. Although a number of common principles seem to underpin many of the specific instances when the law will go behind the corporate veil, these have not been formally acknowledged and there remains a grey area where it may be difficult to assess whether or not protection will be granted. As a result whenever particular reliance is placed upon the company's separate legal persona especially where this is related to the avoidance of some liability it is recommended that legal or accounting advice be sought, as appropriate, to confirm whether or not the separation will be effective.

Advantages of Incorporation

All the advantages (and some of the disadvantages) of incorporation 2.2

flow from the separate legal persona of the company. The advantages can be summarised as follows.

Limited liability

2.2.1 Commercially, one of the main attractions of incorporation is limited liability. Most companies are limited either by shares or by guarantee. Where a company is limited by shares, each member is liable only for the amount, if any, unpaid on the shares which he has agreed to take. If, for example, he buys 100 shares of £1 each and pays over the full purchase price in return for the shares, then he will have no further liability for the company's debts. If, on the other hand, in the example quoted, he pays, in the first instance, only one-half of the amount due on the shares, that is £50, then his liability for the debts of the company will be limited to the balance of £50 remaining due.

Where a company is limited by guarantee, the members each undertake to pay on a specified date or on the happening of a specified event (usually the winding-up of the company) such an amount up to a fixed sum as may be required to settle any outstanding debts of the company. Guarantee companies are commonly, although not invariably, used for charitable purposes.

It used to be possible to create a hybrid company in which the liability of members was limited both by shares and by guarantee. Such companies cannot now be created (see section 1 (4) of the Companies Act 1985) and are not commonly encountered.

In practice in the case of a small private company there is an important qualification to the benefit to members of the company's limited liability. Large creditors such as banks, commercial landlords or finance houses will not deal with a company without being certain that their money is adequately secured. Often this means that the individuals behind the company will be called upon to provide personal guarantees of the company's indebtedness. If the company is wound up and is unable to pay its debts, those involved may be called upon to settle the sums due to the larger creditors not as members of the company but as the company's guarantors. Clearly this may qualify the benefit which would otherwise be obtained from limited liability. As far as those involved with companies are concerned, the granting of such guarantees should be avoided if at all possible even although this may involve investing rather more in the company itself than might otherwise have been wished.

Ordinary trade creditors (or lay people) while they may call for trade references are unlikely to insist upon more. It is they who usually fall foul of the limited liability of the company when it is wound up for insolvency with often little or nothing left after the secured creditors have been paid. There can be no doubt that the privilege of limited liability has often been abused to the prejudice of a company's ordinary creditors. Parliament has endeavoured to strike a balance between continuing to encourage business enterprise, with the promise that an entrepreneur need not be ruined because his best endeavours failed to turn up trumps, and protecting the public from those who use limited liability as a front for fraud and a means of fleecing trade creditors and lay people alike.

Fraudulent trading has long been struck at under section 213 of the Insolvency Act 1986 and its statutory predecessors and this was extended with the introduction of the concept of wrongful trading under section 214 of the Act. As will be examined in Chapter 6 the directors of a company may be held personally liable for the company's debts if they continue to trade knowing that the company is unlikely to be able to pay its debts. Continuing defaulters in respect of the provisions of the Companies Acts and those who have been involved with more than one insolvent company can also be prevented from being involved with companies in the future. These rules have been strengthened by the Insolvency Act 1986 and by the Company Directors Disqualification Act 1986. There is also now provision (under sections 216 and 217 of the Insolvency Act 1986) preventing an individual who was a director or shadow director of a company which has gone into insolvent liquidation from being involved with a company of the same name or with a similar name within a period of five years of the first company going into liquidation. In truth however, despite these provisions, the ordinary creditor is still in an extremely vulnerable position in his dealings with small limited companies.

The other indirect means of protecting creditors is by providing for the publication of details of a company's accounts and its financial and other affairs and the placing of restrictions upon the dissolution and distribution of the company's assets. These will, of course, be dealt with as disadvantages of incorporation.

Tax advantages

Broadly speaking, the taxation of companies is now in line with the taxation of individuals with the basic rate of income tax for individuals currently being fixed at the same rate as the small companies rate for corporation tax (24 per cent). However, higher rate income tax payers who wish to accumulate profits within the business will normally still derive a tax advantage from incorporation. Moreover, incorporation opens the way to issuing or transferring shares to other members of the family, which can be a tax efficient means of transferring wealth. Shares can also be transferred to spouses in certain circumstances to take full advantage of independent taxation. All these opportunities must however be set against the potential disadvantages of incorporation (paragraph 2.3.3 below). 2.2.2

The realm of company taxation is extremely complicated and in all but the most straightforward cases the advice of experienced accountants should be sought prior to incorporation.

Perpetual succession

2.2.3 A company, once formed, exists as a separate legal entity until wound up or struck from the Register either by the court, the Registrar, its members or outraged creditors. It is not "subject to the thousand natural shocks that flesh is heir to" and accordingly it continues regardless of the fates or fortunes of its members who can pass on their shareholdings in the company from one generation to another. This may be of particular relevance where landed families wish to pass on assets from one generation to another in such a manner as to minimise the inheritance tax payable. Shares provide for a more convenient graduated transfer of wealth in that, generally speaking, it is easier for say a farming company with an issued share capital of one million ordinary £1 shares worth £1 each to be transferred by tranches of 100,000, 250,000 or 500,000 shares or whatever than it is for a farm worth £1 million to be transferred to the transferees in portions of one tenth, one-quarter, one-half or whatever. Likewise, a company may be useful as a means of holding property in the name of a trust, club or partnership where the membership of that body changes or may change on a regular basis.

Borrowing

2.2.4 Companies, and companies alone, can grant a special form of security to creditors known as a floating charge. A floating charge is useful in that it enables the company to give security over some or all of its property and assets including not only land and buildings but debts and moveable items such as stock and machinery; such moveable items cannot otherwise be utilised for security purposes without their being delivered into the custody of the creditor or his agent. The company is not prevented from dealing with its assets which, in the general case, are only affected by the charge in the event either of a receiver being appointed, or of the company being wound up. In either of these situations the floating charge is said to crystallise, attaching to all the assets of the company at that time and preventing their being dealt with further. The holder of the floating charge then has a fixed security over the assets covered by the charge. Once again there are often restrictions in practice. The banks or other lending institutions will restrict the extent to which they will lend upon the value of the assets covered by the charge in a way which reflects their lack of control over the company's dealing with these assets. As a general guideline they will perhaps lend only 50 per cent or less of the value of the underlying assets. If further borrowing is required, then they will call for additional security perhaps reverting again to personal guarantees by the parties involved. The lending institution may attempt to impose restrictions upon the company's dealing with its assets by inserting particular provisions into the charge document itself. This may provide, for example, that the company is not at liberty to sell, dispose of or otherwise deal with any asset over a fixed value or which exceeds a certain percentage of the value of the company's assets as a whole.

Investment

The structure of a company is extremely flexible and can usually be 2.2.5
adapted to deal with any particular set of circumstances. Through the system of shareholding it enables individuals, groups or other companies to invest in a business without requiring them to become actively involved in the day-to-day management of the enterprise. This applies not only to large public companies which may be quoted on the London Stock Exchange but also, to a lesser extent, to smaller private companies.

Provided adequate safeguards are incorporated in the company's framework the corporate structure enables one individual to contribute cash to an enterprise while another provides labour or expertise; the investment of each, in cash or in kind, being protected and rewarded. In this area, however, care must be taken by the participants that the corporate structure is not abused to the prejudice of one or more of the parties involved.

The investor will receive shares in return for their investment. In the ordinary case their only return on these shares will be a dividend, generally either at a fixed rate in the case of preferred shares or at a rate varying with distributed profits in the case of ordinary shares. In the case of ordinary shares, however, the directors recommend payment of dividends at a specified level normally on an annual basis (although they may also declare one or more interim dividends throughout the company's financial year), which recommendation is put to the company in general meeting for approval. In terms of Article 102 of Table A, which is normally adopted by companies without modification, the members can only approve or reduce the recommended dividend, they cannot resolve that it be increased. As a result, an investor with a minority shareholding is extremely vulnerable as the directors, who may hold the balance of shares, may decline to recommend any dividend, relying instead upon their salaries as directors to draw an income from the company. The Articles of Association of a private company frequently restrict the right of a member to transfer his shares to a third party without the approval of the directors. For this reason an investor can become locked into a company from which he receives no adequate return.

An investor's only remedy may be to petition the court to wind up the company under section 122 of the Insolvency Act 1986 on the grounds that it would be just and equitable so to do. This may often result in further loss as liquidated stock rarely realises its book value and goodwill and other intangible assets may have to be written off. The investor may also apply to the court for a remedy under section 459 of the Companies Act 1985 if he can show that the company has been, is being or is about to be run in a way which has been, is or will be unfairly prejudicial to members including himself. If the court finds in the investor's favour it may make such an order as it thinks fit having regard to all the circumstances including the investor's own conduct if this is relevant. The order granted may for example provide for the payment of dividends by the company, or provide for the aggrieved individual's shares to be purchased at a fair price. Such actions tend to be complex, time-consuming and, as a result, extremely expensive. In fact the best protection is to try and avoid this situation arising from the start either by avoiding the risk altogether or by incorporating adequate safeguards such as weighted voting rights, rights for particular classes of share or by separate contractual arrangement.

On the other side of the coin is the person with the smart idea who has to rely upon others to fund the development of that idea. Such a person is also in a vulnerable position where they do not have a majority of shares of the company. True, they may be a director but, in terms of section 303 of the Companies Act 1985, directors can be removed from the board by an ordinary resolution of the members of the company which requires only a simple majority. Again they must seek to protect their position perhaps by entering into a separate contractual arrangement such as a director's service contract or securing increased voting rights on a resolution to have them removed as a director or specific class rights for their shares to equal effect.

Clearly this matter is one of considerable complexity. The main point to be aware of, however, is that the company can and should be modelled to suit the exact requirements of the parties involved. We shall deal with this in more detail later.

Pension arrangements

2.2.6 The tax provisions governing pension and life assurance contributions can be more favourable to company employees than they are for self-employed persons. The limit on tax-free contributions for employees is effectively set by the limits on benefits which approved schemes can provide. By contrast, the self-employed face a further constraint in the form of limits on their deductible pension payments as a proportion of taxable earnings. However, the position is much less clear cut as a result of the 1989 Finance Act, which imposed further restrictions on higher earners (whether employed or self-employed).

Disadvantages of Incorporation

As stated, setting up a company may not always be the best way forward for a business. There are a number of disadvantages to incorporation, in particular the following factors should be noted. 2.3

Cost

There are a number of costs which may be incurred in incorporating and running a company. Currently the dues of incorporation, payable to the Registrar of Companies, are £20. An expedited service is available allowing incorporation or a change of name to be effected that day at a cost of £100 in each case. The cost of submitting an annual return is £15 and of changing the company's name £10. Although not now required by law (see section 130 of the Companies Act 1989 substituting new sections 36A and 36B to the Companies Act 1985) a company may wish to obtain a corporate seal which will cost between £30 and £50 depending upon the type ordered. Company books including the various statutory registers to be kept by the company will also require to be made up or purchased at a cost of around £50. Annual accounts must be kept and submitted which will entail both accountants' and perhaps auditors' fees. Legal advice may also be required which will be a further (if worthwhile) drain upon resources. 2.3.1

As a bare minimum it will cost £20 to incorporate a company and, if the company is dormant, £15 per annum thereafter assuming that you do all the paperwork yourself. More realistically it is probably necessary to set aside perhaps £500 for a simple company incorporation and, assuming the company is dormant, perhaps £250 per annum thereafter.

Administration

The Companies Acts and the Articles of Association of a company lay down a detailed procedure for the day-to-day management of the company's affairs. There must be meetings of directors and of members, all of which must be carefully minuted. Registers must be kept of the members, directors, directors' interests in the shares or debentures of the company and of any charges granted by the company. As stated, accounts must be made up and lodged with an annual return of the company's affairs. Failure to comply with the statutory requirements may result in the company and its directors 2.3.2

and officers being fined and even, in extreme cases, in the company being struck from the Register. Even for a dormant company there is an annual routine to be carried through and for a going concern the workload can be considerable.

Taxation and national insurance contributions

2.3.3 As stated, the incorporation of a company can be tax disadvantageous and it will be necessary in most cases to obtain professional advice as to the tax implications of incorporation. In some cases, for example, incorporation may give rise to the possibility of double taxation on profits. Suppose, for example, that a small company is set up with a view to investing in a particular piece of property. The investment is successful and the company derives a substantial profit. The company will pay corporation tax upon this capital gain. If the members then wish to pay out that profit to themselves as individuals, perhaps by winding up the company and distributing its assets, then they may find that they are paying capital gains tax upon the increase in the value of the company's shares which will directly reflect the profits made by the company and which will have already been subject to corporation tax in respect of that gain.

National insurance contributions may also be increased by incorporation, resulting in a further charge which must be set against the advantages noted earlier. Even although an individual substantially owns and runs the company which employs them (wearing the three hats of member, director and employee) both the company and the individual will require to pay their respective Class I contributions. In some cases these disadvantages can be minimised by using dividends as a means of extracting value from the company. There are however a number of other potential disadvantages arising from the detailed rules concerning loss relief and various capital gains and inheritance tax reliefs which must be considered, as too should the effect on pensionable earnings.

Finally, even where incorporation will prove advantageous in the long term, there are likely to be tax costs arising from transferring an existing business into a company. For example, stamp duty is payable at the rate of one per cent on the transfer of certain assets to a company in return for shares.

Disclosure

2.3.4 As mentioned above, one of the protections for the public against the abuse of limited liability is that a company is bound to disclose to its own members, to the Registrar of Companies and in its own statutory registers details of its affairs. Once lodged with the Registrar a company's accounts and returns are available to anyone who wishes information regarding that company. In particular, annual accounts must be lodged. Clearly this may be not only embarrassing but also ruinous; a gift of valuable commercial information to trade creditors. There have been some provisions introduced in recent years so that small and medium-sized companies need not register publicly the full accounts required for larger companies. Such companies must, however, continue to prepare full accounts for issue to their own members and as a result, unless their accounts are viewed as containing particularly sensitive information, many companies continue to register full accounts despite the relaxation of the statutory provisions. In the case of large quoted companies the costs of issuing the annual accounts to all members can be substantial. This is partly alleviated by the provision contained in section 15 of the Companies Act 1989 which sanctions the issue of a summary financial statement in place of full accounts provided that the summary meets a number of specific requirements.

Withdrawal of capital

The Companies Act 1985 as amended contains numerous 2.3.5
restrictions on the distribution and dissolution of a company's capital and its use for certain purposes, for example the making of loans to directors or the purchase by the company of its own shares. This means that, once incorporated, a business cannot be treated by its owners as it was before. They can no longer simply withdraw money as if it were their own — it isn't; it is the company's and they can only get at and use that money by complying with the terms of the Companies Acts.

Conclusion

It will be readily gathered from the above that the decision whether 2.4
or not to set up and use a company is far from a simple or straightforward one. In general the problem will have to be approached from three different standpoints; legal, accounting and commercial. Professional advice can generally be obtained on the first two aspects of incorporation; the third must always remain a matter for the participants themselves.

CHAPTER 3

INCORPORATION

General

3.1 The incorporation of a company is, in itself, fairly straightforward. The advisability of incorporation on the other hand or the exact structure of the company to be used is far more complex and, in all but the most simple cases, will require detailed legal and other professional advice. The purpose of this chapter, however, is to deal with the process of incorporation. I will begin with a general outline of the documents involved.

Memorandum of Association

3.2 The Memorandum of Association is the founding document of the company. In terms of section 1 of the Companies Act 1985 any person may, by subscribing a Memorandum of Association and otherwise complying with the Act, set up a limited company. Since 1992 it has been possible to establish a private company with one member only. Prior to then at least two members were required. This resulted in a number of companies having one share held by a nominee of the principal owner who held all the remaining shares. The Memorandum must state:

(a) the name of the company;
(b) the country in which the registered office is situated;
(c) the objects of the company;
(d) a statement that the liability of members is limited; and
(e) details of the capital structure of the company (or in the case of a company limited by guarantee, details of the amount which the members undertake to guarantee).

The Memorandum will close with a subscription clause (the declaration of association) whereby the subscriber or subscribers confirm their desire to incorporate a company in terms of the Memorandum and, in the case of a company limited by shares, agree to take a specified number of shares in the company so created. The signatures of subscribers require to be witnessed by a single witness only.

Section 3 of the 1985 Act provides that the Memorandum should be as near as circumstances permit to the statutory style laid down from time to time by the Secretary of State. This is currently contained in The Companies (Tables A to F) Regulations 1985 (S.I. 1985 No. 805 as amended by S.I. 1985 No. 1052) and, in particular, Table B thereof in the case of a private company limited by shares. The style in the case of a company limited by guarantee is contained in Table C. While this general statutory requirement should always be borne in mind the style of Memorandum currently used by most companies and, in particular the objects clause thereof, is considerably more extensive than the statutory style might suggest. This has largely been accepted as a result of common usage and practice. Notwithstanding this further substantial deviation should be avoided.

Company name

Sections 25 and 26 of the 1985 Act and the Business Names Act 1985 contain a number of restrictions upon the names which can be used for limited companies. In particular, the following rules should be noted. 3.2.1

(a) The company name must end with the word "Limited" or a short or Welsh form thereof. The word "Limited" must not appear elsewhere in the company name. In the case of companies limited by guarantee it is possible (in terms of section 30 of the 1985 Act) to obtain exemption from the Secretary of State from the use of the word "Limited." Strict criteria require to be met before such an exemption will be afforded, namely:

- (i) the objects of the company as set out in the Memorandum of Association must be the promotion of commerce, art, science, education, religion, charity or any profession and any thing incidental or conducive to any of these objects;
- (ii) the profits and other income of the company must be applied in promoting the objects of the company;
- (iii) the Articles of Association must expressly exclude the payment of dividends to the members; and
- (iv) the Memorandum of Association must contain a provision to the effect that in the event of the company being wound up its assets shall be transferred, not to its members, but to another body with objects of a charitable nature or similar to its own and with similar prohibitions on the distribution of its profits and assets.

If, once the exemption is obtained, the company alters its Memorandum or Articles of Association or simply fails to comply with their terms so that it no longer complies with the statutory criteria then the Secretary of State has power to require the company to include the word "Limited" in its name. Typically the exemption is sought by charities who wish to operate through a company. Clearly it would not be appropriate for a company operating in the usual commercial sense. To obtain the exemption, a statutory declaration indicating compliance with the statutory criteria should be submitted in the prescribed form (Form 30 (5) (a)) to the Registrar. Once the exemption is granted a company does not need to use the word "Limited" on its seal, cheques or letter heads. This advantage, if such it can be called, is partly offset by the requirement (contained in section 351 of the Act) that a company so exempt must disclose that fact on its notepaper. Dispensation from the use of the word "Limited" may also be sought after incorporation, provided the company applying complies with similar criteria to those noted above.

(b) The name must not be the same as, or similar to, an existing company's name. If the name of a company already in existence sounds like the name proposed for a new company the Registrar may reject the proposed name. In order to ascertain whether or not a name will be available it is possible to do a company name search either by checking the Register of Companies or by using private company searchers. A name cannot be reserved however and accordingly any delay between the checking of a name's availability and the subsequent submission of incorporation forms should be minimised. Even if the Registrar of Companies finds a name acceptable and issues a certificate of incorporation in that name the company is not thereby protected from a "passing off" action raised by a third party. Such an action may be raised where the third party feels that the company's name is so similar to that of the third party that the two are likely to be confused. The third party would require to show however that the company (or, more appropriately, the individuals concerned with it) had acted with an intent to deceive or mislead the public.

(c) The name must not, in the opinion of the Secretary of State, constitute a criminal offence or be offensive. Various statutes prohibit the use of certain words in a company name and failure to observe such prohibitions may constitute a criminal offence. The Registrar may request confirmation that the use of a particular word does not contravene the relevant legislation. An illustrative (but not exhaustive) list of such words and the addresses of the body to whom requests should be made for such confirmation is contained in Schedules 2 and 3.

(d) The name must not suggest a link with the government or local authority or, without appropriate approval, contain a word included in the regulations passed under section 29 of the Companies Act 1985. If, for example, a company was to be set up incorporating as part of its name the words "Angus County" the Registrar of Companies might require, prior to registration, confirmation from Angus County Council that it consented to the company's proposed name. Likewise, in terms of the Company and Business Names Regulations 1981 (S.I. 1981 No. 1685) certain words require the consent of a specific body if they are to be used in a company name. A list of the words covered by these regulations and the bodies whose approval is required is contained in Schedule 2. Again a letter from the appropriate body confirming that they approve of the use of the word and have no objection to its forming part of the name of the company should be obtained and forwarded to the Registrar of Companies together with the other incorporation papers.

In addition to these specific restrictions there is a general prohibition on the use of a name which is misleading. For example a small private retail company operating from a corner shop in Edinburgh could not call itself the International Trading Company Limited. A company wishing to use the word "international" in its name will normally require to satisfy the Registrar that it will be trading with at least two other nations.

As we will see, following incorporation, a company can change its name by special resolution under section 28 of the 1985 Act. In addition, the Secretary of State can compel a company to change its name if it is misleading or if it clashes with the name of another company on the Register.

Registered office

Every company must have a registered office in terms of section 287 of the 1985 Act (as amended by section 136 of the Companies Act 1989). The initial location of a company's registered office must be stated on Companies Form 10 which is submitted to the Registrar of Companies as part of the incorporation procedure. For a company incorporated in England or Wales, the registered office must be in England or Wales. Likewise a company incorporated in Scotland must have its registered office in Scotland. In the Memorandum of Association it is only necessary to specify the country in which the registered office will be situated. Any change of the registered office can only be within the boundaries of the country of registration and is effected by intimation to the Registrar using Companies Form 287. The change is effective on registration of the required form by the Registrar. Documents may, however, continue to be served on the former registered office during the period of 14 days following such registration. 3.2.2

Objects clause

It is stating the obvious to say that this clause specifies the objects for which the company is incorporated. It also has the effect of restricting the activities in which the company can engage. The 3.2.3

company is only empowered to undertake such activities as are specified in the Memorandum of Association and attempts to engage in any business outwith this scope are deemed to be outwith the power of the company — such unauthorised activity is said to be *ultra vires* (literally "beyond the powers") of the company. The principle upon which this rule was founded was, and is, a reasonable one, namely that it would be unfair to a member of a company who had agreed to invest in the company on the understanding that it was to take over an existing and well-established retail business to discover that, without any authority, the company was now engaging in highly speculative property developments.

Accordingly, if the objects of a company define its business as that of garage proprietors, it ought not to engage in the business of running a casino. Formerly, attempts by the company to validate such actings would be ineffective even if every member subsequently approved the change of business (*Ashbury Railway Carriage and Iron Co. v. Riche* (1875) L.R. 7 H.L. 653). This provision has now been altered by section 108 of the Companies Act 1989 (amending section 35 of the 1985 Act) which allows for ratification of *ultra vires* acts by special resolution of the members of the company. Alternatively, *prior* to commencing the operation of the casino, the members of the company might resolve by special resolution to amend the objects of the company to include the new business. The company would then be acting within its powers, that is *intra vires.*

3.2.4 The statutory style of Memorandum of Association contained in Table B gives the following as an example of an objects clause: "The company's objects are the carriage of passengers and goods in motor vehicles between such places as the company may from time to time determine and the doing of such other things as are incidental or conducive to the attainment of that object."

Unfortunately, the modern objects clause normally extends to several pages narrating not only the main objects of the company but also the powers which the company is to have to enable it to carry out those objects. In the example given above the company set up principally to carry on business as garage proprietors may well, on paper at least, have power to operate a casino. This arose as a result of the *ultra vires* rule whereby any act by a company outwith its expressed objects might be struck down not only by third parties but by the company itself. This rule has been substantially restricted by the Companies Act 1989. Nevertheless it continues to be of importance and, to avoid its adverse effects, it is common to find in the objects clause not only the main objects of the company but also every additional object or power which the company might wish to rely upon in the future.

The objects clause generally takes the form of a series of numbered paragraphs. The first of these will usually set out in some detail the main object or objects of the company. This will be followed by a "catch-all" clause which will provide that the company can carry on any other trade or business which, in the opinion of the directors, can be conveniently or advantageously carried on in association with the main objects. The remainder of the paragraphs will normally simply enumerate various powers (as opposed to objects) which the company will be able to exercise in the carrying out or attaining of its objects. The clause will normally end with an express statement that each of the paragraphs is to be interpreted and treated as if it were a separate object of the company and that no paragraph is to be limited by reference to the other paragraphs or by reference to the name of the company.

In terms of section 3A of the Companies Act 1985, which was introduced by section 110 of the 1989 Act, a company may now state in its Memorandum that its object is to carry on business as a general commercial company. In this event the company is, in terms of the Act, empowered to carry on any trade, business or profession whatsoever and to do all such things as are incidental or conducive to the carrying on of any trade or business by it. This section has been widely but not universally adopted in new company formations and some existing companies have adopted the form of object clause suggested by the section. While the Act might be thought to dispense with the requirement to repeat the various powers usually narrated in objects clauses, lawyers have generally continued to narrate all or at least some of these being nervous to exclude these until the exact import of the Act is known. Some powers may not be deemed to be "incidental or conducive" to a trade or business and these will require to be specifically stated. For example the power to grant guarantees or other securities for the obligations of another company may require express authority. Likewise the sale of the business of the company may not be viewed as "incidental or conducive" to that business.

As stated, usually only the first and second paragraphs will state what can really be regarded as the objects of the company with the remainder of the paragraphs in the objects clause simply narrating powers to be available to the company. This distinction between objects and powers is important. It has been established in a number of cases that many of the powers contained in the objects clause cannot be exercised in isolation without reference to the main objects of the company. This remains the case notwithstanding the general proviso which usually appears at the end of the objects clause and which is noted above. In the case of *Introductions* [1969] 1 All E.R. 887, for example it was held that although a company had power to borrow money in terms of its Memorandum it could do so only in so far as this was required or connected with the main object of the company as specified in the first paragraph of its objects clause.

For this reason also great care should be taken before relying on a general provision such as that quoted above that the company can carry on any business that the directors deem to be advantageous or convenient. Although there is some judicial authority supporting such clauses there is a danger that the courts will hold such a clause as being too widely drawn to be viewed as an object at all.

Historical application of the *ultra vires* rule

3.2.5 As stated above, a company which acts outwith its objects clause is deemed to act *ultra vires*. Formerly, this had a number of repercussions not only for the company itself but for those dealing with it. The company would not be able to sue upon any purported contract falling outwith the objects of the company. It was a valid defence in any such action raised by the company that the contract was *ultra vires*. Likewise, the company could defend an action raised by a third party in terms of a purported contract on the grounds that the contract itself was *ultra vires*. In this way companies were able to use the *ultra vires* rule to the prejudice of third parties who had contracted with them in good faith. For example, in the case of *Re Jon Beauforte (London) Ltd* [1953] 1 All E.R. 634, coal merchants supplied coal to a company to enable it to manufacture veneer panels. It subsequently transpired that the company was not empowered in terms of its Memorandum to carry on such a business. The company was wound up and the coal merchant sought to recover the value of the coal delivered to the company. It was held that he could not do so as his contract with the company was *ultra vires*. It is worthy of note that the coal merchant was deemed to have notice of the contents of the company's Memorandum which had, of course, been registered with the Registrar of Companies. He should, in other words, have been aware of the position. The principle of deemed notice has now been abolished by section 142 of the 1989 Act.

Clearly this position was most inequitable and relief was finally given to third parties by virtue of section 9 (1) of the European Communities Act 1972. This was re-enacted as section 35 of the Companies Act 1985. Unfortunately, the protection originally afforded by this section was not as extensive as might have been hoped. Firstly, the transaction had to be decided upon "by the directors". It was not clear whether a transaction entered into by one of the directors or by a managing director on behalf of the company would be covered by the section. To minimise this risk those dealing with a company often requested an excerpt, certified as correct, from the minute of the board meeting approving the obtaining of a loan, the granting of a security or any other transaction being entered into by the company. Secondly, the third party had to be acting in good faith although there was a presumption in their favour to this effect.

Present application of the *ultra vires* rule

Section 108 of the 1989 Act replaced the former section 35 of the 1985 Act and introduced two further sections numbered 35A and 35B. These provisions may be summarised as follows. 3.2.6

(a) The validity of an act done by a company is not now to be called into question on the ground of lack of capacity by reason of anything in the company's Memorandum.

(b) Notwithstanding the foregoing, a member of a company may bring proceedings to restrain an act which, but for the foregoing provision, would be outwith the powers of the company unless it is done in fulfilment of a legal obligation arising from a previous act of the company. For example, if a company has contracted to sell property, the shareholders may be unable to prevent implementation of that contract by completion of the sale.

(c) Directors have a duty to respect any limitation on their powers flowing from the Memorandum or otherwise. Acts outwith the powers of the directors may be ratified by special resolution of the shareholders but if directors or others are to be relieved from any liability arising from a breach of this duty a further special resolution is required.

(d) Providing that a person dealing with a company acts in good faith, the power of the board of directors to bind the company or to authorise others to do so is deemed to be free from any limitation in terms of the company's constitution. As before, third parties are deemed to act in good faith unless the contrary is shown. Interestingly, showing that a third party knew an act to be outwith the power of the directors is not in itself conclusive of bad faith — one wonders what is. There is no obligation on third parties to investigate whether or not directors have power to enter a specific transaction. Again these provisions do not affect the rights of shareholders against directors of the company.

As stated, despite the substantial alterations introduced by the 1989 Act, the *ultra vires* rule continues to be of relevance. If directors act outwith the objects clause they may find themselves liable to the members of the company for any loss sustained as a result. It is therefore essential for the directors of a company and for their legal advisers to be fully acquainted with the contents of the Memorandum and Articles of Association in order to ensure that this problem does not arise.

Alteration of objects

As we will see, it is possible to alter the objects of a company by a special resolution in terms of section 4 of the Companies Act 1985. This will be dealt with in more detail later. 3.2.7

Limited liability

3.2.8 This clause simply states that the liability of the members is limited. Clearly this would be inappropriate in an unlimited company. It is possible in terms of section 49 of the Companies Act 1985 for a limited company to become an unlimited company by lodging Companies Form 49 (1) if all the members of the company agree (the members being required to sign Companies Form 49 (8) (d)). Equally, an unlimited company can become a limited company by passing a special resolution in terms of section 51 of the Companies Act 1985, the relevant form being Companies Form 51. In this case, however, protection is provided for creditors who clearly might otherwise be prejudiced.

Whilst it is possible therefore in terms of the Companies Act 1985 for limited companies to register as unlimited and vice versa it should be noted that statute does not authorise the re-registration of companies limited by shares as companies limited by guarantee or vice versa. As a point of interest there is a provision in the Companies Act 1985 (section 307) which provides that a limited company may, if authorised by its Articles of Association, alter its Memorandum of Association by special resolution to the effect that the liability of its directors or managers or of any managing director is unlimited. This provision is rarely used.

Capital clause

3.2.9 This clause will specify the capital structure of the company. In the case of a company limited by shares, it will specify the number, value and type (*e.g.* ordinary and/or preferred or otherwise) of shares which the company is to have available for issue to members. This is referred to as the company's nominal or unauthorised share capital. In the case of a guarantee company, this clause will specify the maximum amount to be contributed by each member on the happening of a specified event, normally the winding up of the company. The amount which the members of a guarantee company undertake to contribute is usually a nominal amount arbitrarily selected, *e.g.* £1.00 or £5.00 unless (and unusually) the company is being incorporated solely for commercial purposes rather than for philanthropic reasons. In this case, the members might find that for the purpose of maintaining credibility in the eyes of the company's future creditors they require to set the guarantee level at a higher figure.

Declaration of Association

3.2.10 The Declaration of Association is simply a statement by the subscriber or subscribers of the memorandum, who on incorporation will be the first member(s) of the company, that they wish to form the company and, in the case of a company limited by shares, that they wish to subscribe for the number of shares which are set out in their own hand alongside their signature(s). Each subscriber should sign their usual signature. The Registrar may not accept a memorandum in which the number of shares subscribed for is shown in typeface or print *unless* the subscribers are only subscribing for one share each. The total number of shares subscribed for should also be stated unless this is only one.

Subscribers may subscribe for more than one share and indeed there is no reason in law why the entire authorised share capital should not be subscribed for at that time although it is customary for subscribers simply to subscribe for one share each and to apply for the balance of their proposed share holdings after incorporation.

The above constitutes nothing more than a summary of the main aspects of the Memorandum of Association. As stated, this document will often extend to several pages. Schedule 4 contains a style which is generally sufficient for most companies. The main object or objects of the company would be inserted in paragraph 3 (1). A style Memorandum for a guarantee company with charitable objects is provided in Schedule 5. Samples of main objects clauses are also provided in Schedule 6.

Articles of Association

The Articles of Association form the framework for the day-to-day management of a company. They are subservient to the Memorandum of Association in that they cannot give to the company any power which is outwith the company's Memorandum of Association. The Articles will however normally specify how the powers of the company are to be exercised. As we shall see the Articles lie at the heart of the relationship between the various members of the company and between the company's shareholders and its directors. 3.3

In terms of section 14 of the Companies Act 1985, the Memorandum and Articles of Association when registered bind the company and its members as if they had each entered a contract with the others agreeing to be bound by the terms of the Memorandum and Articles of Association. This is of particular relevance with regard to the Articles. In the case of *Eley v. Positive Government Security Life Association* [1876] 1 Ex.D.88, C.A. 89, a company was incorporated with Articles of Association which provided for the appointment of Mr Eley as the company's solicitor. Following incorporation however the board of the company decided to utilise the services of another solicitor. Mr Eley raised an action for damages on the ground of a breach of the contract contained in the Articles of Association. In this case it was held that Mr Eley's claim must fail. He was endeavouring to enforce the Articles not as a member of the company but in his capacity as a solicitor; in which capacity he was effectively an outsider. This somewhat strange decision was based upon the English doctrine of privity of contract. In Scotland this case might well have been decided differently as Scots law accepts that where two or more persons contract together with a view to benefiting another, that third party can sue on the basis of the respective undertakings or promises contained in the contract for their benefit.

In terms of section 7 of the Companies Act 1985, a company limited by shares *may* register Articles of Association. A company limited by guarantee or an unlimited company *must* register Articles of Association. The Articles must be printed (typewritten will suffice) and be divided into consecutively numbered paragraphs. They must be signed by each subscriber to the Memorandum of Association in the presence of a single witness.

In terms of section 8 of the Companies Act 1985, the Secretary of State may prescribe regulations giving styles for the Articles of Association of a company. These styles are generally referred to as Tables A, C, D and E and the current styles are contained in the Companies (Tables A–F) Regulations 1985 (S.I. 1985 No. 805) as amended by the Companies (Tables A–F) (Amendment) Regulations 1985 (S.I. 1985 No. 1052). Section 128 of the Companies Act 1989 enables the Secretary of State to prescribe Articles of Association appropriate for "a partnership company"; that is a company limited by shares whose shares are intended to be held to a substantial extent by, or on behalf of, its employees. As yet no such Articles have been published although the Department of Trade and Industry have produced a consultative document. The table most commonly referred to is Table A which contains regulations for the management of a company limited by shares. If a company registered by shares does not register Articles of Association or does not exclude or modify Table A, that table, so far as applicable and in force at the date of the company's incorporation, will constitute the company's Articles of Association. It should be noted therefore that where a company limited by shares adopts Table A, either expressly or by implication and whether in whole or in part it will, unless the contrary is expressly provided, be the Table A applicable at the date of its incorporation. In dealing with such a company it is important to establish which Table A applies. Subsequent alterations to Table A will not affect a company incorporated prior to the date of such alterations taking effect. The Articles of Association for companies limited by guarantee and for unlimited companies are specified in Tables C, D and E which are currently contained in the statutory instruments noted above.

Despite the relaxations available to companies limited by shares, almost all companies choose to register Articles of Association which to a greater or lesser extent modify, amend or replace the provisions of Table A. We shall examine some of the more important provisions in the following sections.

Alteration of Articles

As we shall see in Chapter 8, a company may, in terms of section 9 of the Companies Act 1985, alter its Articles of Association by special resolution. This will be dealt with in more detail later. 3.3.1

Principal Articles and amendments to Table A

As stated above, most companies adopt the current Table A subject to a number of amendments. A copy of the current Table A is contained in Schedule 7 and a copy of abbreviated Articles based upon, but amending, Table A is contained in Schedule 8. It would be unusual for a company to operate on the basis of Table A without any amendments or alterations. In each case the Articles should be tailored to meet the precise needs of the company and its participants. This may mean deviating substantially from the standard provisions contained in the Schedule and detailed legal advice should be sought in any such case. The purpose of the following paragraphs is simply to outline the principal provisions which ordinarily apply to private limited companies and to highlight some of the more common amendments and alterations. 3.3.2

Share capital — Articles 2–4 of Table A

The articles referred to contain the standard provisions regarding the share capital of the company and, in particular, enable the company to issue different classes of shares including redeemable shares. In terms of section 80 of the Companies Act 1985 the directors of a company are not entitled to issue "relevant securities" unless authorised to do so either by an ordinary resolution of the company or by the company's Articles of Association. "Relevant securities" are defined to include all shares other than subscriber shares or shares allotted in pursuance of an employee share scheme and include any options to acquire shares or to convert a security into shares. The authority given may be either conditional or unconditional and must state the maximum period, not exceeding five years from either the date of the resolution or the adoption of the relevant article, within which it may be exercised. The authority may be renewed from time to time as appropriate. Provided that the authority is appropriately worded, the directors may be permitted to allot relevant securities after the expiry of the period of the authority in implement of an obligation arising prior to the date of such expiry. It is interesting to 3.3.3

note that any resolution passed in terms of section 80 may be passed by an ordinary resolution notwithstanding that it may affect the Articles of Association of the company. In each case however, a certified copy of the resolution must be passed to the Registrar of Companies within 15 days.

In the case of private companies, it is now open to the shareholders (in terms of section 80A of the 1985 Act as inserted by section 115 of the 1989 Act) to elect by elective resolution that the authority of the directors to allot shares should subsist for a stated period, even if more than five years, or for an indefinite period. The procedure for an elective resolution will be considered in Chapter 5.

Sections 89–96 of the Companies Act 1985 contain statutory pre-emption rights in favour of the existing members of a company on the allotment of shares in that company. In terms of the statutory provisions, a company proposing to allot "equity securities" must first offer such securities to each person who holds relevant shares or relevant employee shares in proportion, as nearly as practicable, to the shareholdings currently held by them. The statutory provisions do not apply to an allotment of equity securities if these are, or are to be, wholly or partly paid up otherwise than in cash, or if they are to be held under an employee share scheme. Equity securities for the purposes of the statutory provisions include any shares other than subscriber shares, bonus shares, shares granted in pursuance of an employee share scheme or shares which carry a right to participate only up to a specified amount in respect of a distribution of dividends or capital.

The sections referred to contain detailed provisions which should be carefully studied prior to the issue of any shares in the share capital of the company. In summary however, the statutory procedure to be followed if a company wishes to allot shares is as follows:

(a) the shares must first be offered in writing to each existing holder of relevant shares either personally or by sending it by post to the member at their registered address. In the case of joint holders the offer should be made to the holder first named in the Register of Members. In the case of the death or bankruptcy of a member, the offer should be made to their executor, trustee or other appropriate representative;

(b) the offer must state a period of not less than 21 days within which it may be accepted and the offer must not be withdrawn prior to the end of that period;

(c) if the member or members in question accept the company's offer then the shares must be allotted to them in terms of the offer. The offer must be on the same or more favourable terms than those upon which the company initially proposed issuing the shares; and

(d) if no acceptances are received or if acceptances are received in respect of only part of the shares proposed to be issued, then the

> company may proceed to allot the whole or that part of the shares not taken up by the existing members of the company.

In terms of section 95 of the Act, the statutory pre-emption rights may be effectively waived by the members of a company. If the directors of the company have been generally authorised to allot shares in the share capital of the company, for the purposes of section 80 of the Act they may be given power either in terms of the Articles of Association of the company or in terms of a special resolution of the company to allot such shares as if the statutory pre-emption rights did not apply to the company. This authority may be renewed in the same manner as the authority granted under section 80.

As a result of the foregoing statutory provisions, it is common for private limited companies to amend the Articles of Association first to enable the directors to allot shares in the company and secondly authorising them to do so without regard to the statutory pre-emption rights noted above. Article 4 of the amended Articles of Association contained in Schedule 8 contains a style for this type of clause. Alternatively authority can be given in a single special resolution of the company along the following lines:

> "That the directors of the company be and are hereby generally and unconditionally authorised by the purposes of Section 80 of the Companies Act 1985 to issue the unissued shares in the share capital of the company and that without regard to any rights of pre-emption contained within the Articles of Association of the company or the terms of Sections 89 and 90 of the said Act. The foregoing authority shall subsist for a period of five years following the date of adoption of this resolution."

When considering the allotment of shares, it is essential to bear in mind that (except in the case of an elective resolution for an extended period) any authority granted either in the Articles of Association or in a resolution along the lines indicated will expire after a period of five years or such shorter term as may be specified.

While the granting of such authority is relatively common, it may give rise to difficulties where the directors and members of a company are not the same individuals. The authority gives to the directors a considerable power which might enable them to "water down" the holding of an existing member by issuing further shares to one or more individuals. For this reason where the members and directors of a company are not the same, it is prudent to restrict any authority granted either by reference to the number of shares which may be allotted by the directors or by imposing conditions upon allotment. In terms of Article 4, referred to above, the directors are authorised to allot shares up to the company's authorised share capital but such a right is stated to be subject to the rights of pre-emption set out in the Article. The conditions specified are in substitution for the statutory requirements which are expressly excluded. They reduce the period within which an offer must be accepted and provide that members may apply for and take up additional shares, over and above their proportionate entitlement, if these are not taken up by other members.

Trust holding — Article 5 of Table A

3.3.4 In terms of this Article the company is prevented from recognising that any share is held in any trust capacity except as may be specified by law or in the Articles themselves. There are occasions when it may be useful to recognise trust holdings and accordingly this article is sometimes deleted particularly in the case of Scottish companies.

Share certificates, liens and calls — Articles 6–22 of Table A

3.3.5 The foregoing articles are commonly adopted either without modification or with only minor alterations. It may be appropriate however to remove the restriction on the company's lien contained in Article 8 whereby such lien applies only to partly paid shares by deleting the first words appearing in parenthesis. A further amendment to this article will enable the company to claim a lien even in respect of sums which may not be directly related to the shares themselves. Article 15 may also be amended to enable the company to claim expenses in relation to any unpaid call. These alterations are, however, relatively unimportant particularly as the Articles relating to liens and calls are rarely relied upon in practice.

Transfer of shares — Article 23–28 of Table A

3.3.6 Perhaps the most common amendment to the Articles of Association of a private limited company relates to the imposition of restrictions upon the transfer of shares. Article 24 gives to the directors of a company limited rights to refuse to register a transfer of shares particularly if these are partly paid. In the case of fully paid shares however the restrictions are technical in nature only. As the management and operation of most small companies is entirely dependent upon the continued good relations between the members of the company to such a degree that such companies are often no more than partnerships clothed with a corporate form, it is normally essential for the members or directors of the company to place strict controls upon the transfer of shares. These controls generally take the form of the granting of pre-emption rights in favour of the existing members of the company analogous to the statutory pre-emption rights applying on the allotment of shares which were discussed above. The style of such "Transfer Articles" as they are commonly called varies greatly but a typical example is contained in Article 9 of the abbreviated Articles of Association contained in Schedule 8. Generally a procedure is established whereby any member wishing to transfer his shares must first give notice to the company which notice automatically constitutes the company as that member's agent for the purposes of first offering the shares to the existing members of the company in proportion to their respective shareholdings. By this means, the balance between the members is safeguarded, assuming always that the members in question can raise the necessary capital to acquire the shares offered. It is not proposed in the present work to examine the detailed procedure as there are a large number of variations in the various styles of Transfer Articles encountered. Three points may however be usefully noted.

(a) If a transfer of shares is anticipated or if the directors of a company receive notice from a member of his intention to transfer shares then immediate reference should be made to the company's Articles of Association and great care should be taken to ensure that the required procedure is carefully adhered to.

(b) Perhaps the most common source of dispute between a member wishing to transfer his shares and the other members or directors of a company relates to the valuation of the shares which it is proposed to transfer. Generally Transfer Articles will provide for the valuation of the shares in question by the auditors of the company or by an independent expert in cases where the parties cannot themselves agree a fair valuation. Careful regard will require to be paid to the exact terms upon which any such valuation is to be carried out. In particular it should be specified whether the valuation is to take account of the number of shares which it is intended to transfer. If no account is taken of the number of shares to be transferred then each share will be valued, in the ordinary case, as a proportion of the net asset value of the company at the relevant time. If, however, the number of shares to be transferred is taken into account then shares comprised in a minority holding will, in the ordinary case, be worth substantially less than shares comprised in a holding which gives control of the company. Generally the thresholds which have a bearing on this question are those constituting 25 per cent or more of the issued share capital (which would enable the member to block the passing of any special resolution) and a majority holding (which would enable the member to effectively control the company's affairs). Clearly a valuation without regard to the number of shares will favour a minority shareholder.

(c) Again referring to valuation, it may be important to consider whether or not the valuation should be by reference to assets alone, perhaps even assuming a fictitious winding-up of the company, or whether the valuation should be on the basis that the company is a going concern taking account of profits earned from year to year. Generally the latter form is more satisfactory, as a valuation by reference to assets alone may unfairly prejudice the transferor. There may be circumstances however where an asset-based valuation is appropriate where, for example, the departure of the member concerned is likely to have material effect on the company's profitability.

Transmission of shares — Articles 29–31 of Table A

3.3.7 The foregoing provisions apply on the death or bankruptcy of a member of the company. Although these are generally acceptable it may be desirable in smaller companies to include a provision whereby an executor, trustee or other representative wishing to be registered as a member of the company in succession to the deceased or bankrupt member is deemed to give a transfer notice to the company so that the appropriate Transfer Article then comes into operation. A provision such as Article 10 of the short form of Articles in Schedule 8 may be of particular use in the case of small private companies operating as quasi-partnerships where an individual, for whatever reason, ceases to be involved in the management of the company.

Alteration of share capital — Articles 32–34 of Table A

3.3.8 These provisions reflect the statutory requirements for the alteration of the share capital of a company. These Articles are normally adopted without amendment.

Purchase of own shares — Article 35 of Table A

3.3.9 In terms of Chapter VII of Part V of the Companies Act 1985 a company may now, in certain specified circumstances, acquire its own shares (or redeem any redeemable shares) provided that, inter alia, authority is given in the Articles of Association of the company. In the case of a public company such acquisition or redemption can only be made out of distributable profits of the company or the proceeds of a fresh issue of shares. In the case of a private company however, acquisition or redemption may be made out of any monies available to the company provided that the statutory procedure is carefully adhered to and provided that suitable authority is given in the Articles of Association. Article 35 of Table A gives the authority required in each case. The statutory provisions should be carefully referred to and detailed legal and accounting advice should be taken if any such purchase or redemption is proposed as a number of legal and taxation consequences may arise.

Company meetings — Articles 36–63 of Table A

3.3.10 The provisions noted contain detailed regulations for the management of meetings of members of the company. Generally these are adopted with only minor amendments. These Articles will be discussed in more detail later but, in the meantime, three specific points may be noted.

(a) In terms of Article 50 of Table A, in the event of an equality of votes on any resolution, the chairman of the company is entitled to an additional or casting vote. Where the shareholding in the company is split equally between two individuals, families or companies, this additional or casting vote would effectively give control of the company to the individual, family or company which controlled the chair. For this reason it is common to exclude the chairman's casting vote in the situations noted. This exclusion does however give rise to the possibility of a stalemate between the two members or groups of members. If this is a concern then it may be possible to make provision within the Articles in an attempt to prevent such a situation arising. It may, for example, be possible to appoint an independent arbiter to adjudicate on any dispute which may arise with such an arbiter perhaps holding one or more shares enabling him to give effect to his decision. Alternatively a separate agreement may be entered into, regulating the procedure to be followed between the parties in the event of a dispute arising. One example of these so-called "deadlock provisions" is contained in Schedule 9.

(b) The standard provisions provide for each member having a single vote on a show of hands and, on a poll, a single vote for each share held. It may be necessary in a number of situations to give to members weighted or additional voting rights in relation to specific matters. Perhaps the most common amendment arises where there are one or more minority shareholders who are either directors of the company or who nominate directors of the company. Because of the statutory provision whereby any director of a company may be removed by an ordinary resolution it is essential that such a minority member be able to protect either himself or his nominated director from such removal. Following upon the case of *Bushell v. Faith* [1970] A.C. 1099, it has been established that the statutory provision may be circumvented by giving to the member in question additional voting rights on any such resolution. It is therefore common to find provision that on a resolution being put to remove a director that director (or the member nominating him or her) shall have two or more votes for each ordinary share held by him. Where such provisions are required they are now commonly dealt with either by the allotment of separate classes of shares with specific rights for each class or by separate contractual arrangement between the parties.

(c) As will be seen later, the directors enjoy considerable authority in the day to day running of a company and control, in particular, the distribution of profits to the members of the company. For this reason, it may be essential to protect the interests of a minority shareholder by protecting his position either as director of the company or the position of any director nominated by that member. In addition to the amendment noted above, it may be necessary to include a provision whereby certain decisions require the approval of all the members of the company or whereby a minority member is entitled to weighted or additional votes on particular resolutions. Matters which may require to be considered in this regard include the sale of part or the whole of the assets of the business, any alteration to the Memorandum or Articles of Association of the company, any decision regarding the remuneration of the directors of a company, the payment of dividends to the members of the company and any decision regarding the transfer or allotment of shares in the share capital of the company. Again these matters may also be dealt with by attaching specific rights to different classes of shares or by separate contractual arrangement.

Number of directors — Article 64 of Table A

3.3.11 In terms of this Article the number of directors of the company shall be subject to a minimum of two. In terms of section 282 of the Companies Act 1985, a private company or a company registered prior to November 1, 1929, need have only one director. Clearly if a private company wishes to operate with a single director, the standard Article 64 will require to be altered accordingly or an ordinary resolution will require to be passed in terms of the Article. Generally, however, it is recommended that companies operate with a minimum of two directors to avoid difficulties arising on the death, incapacity or unavoidable absence of a sole director.

Alternate directors — Articles 65–69 of Table A

3.3.12 The above numbered Articles contain the standard provisions for the appointment of an alternate director; that is a director appointed to act in the place of an existing director of the company. This may prove a useful device in certain limited circumstances such as the unavoidable absence of a director from board meetings for an extended period. The regular or continued appointment of alternate directors should, however, be avoided if possible.

Directors' powers — Articles 70–72 of Table A

3.3.13 Article 70 of Table A lies at the very heart of the legal relationship between the members and directors of a limited company. In terms of this provision the directors are given authority to manage the business of the company and to exercise all the powers of the company, subject only to any relevant statutory provisions, the Memorandum and Articles of Association of the company and to any directions given by the members of the company by way of special resolution. No act of the directors can be invalidated by a subsequent alteration of the Memorandum or Articles of Association or by any subsequent special resolution. The directors are further authorised to appoint agents or attorneys and to delegate their powers to one or more of their number or to any managing director or any other director holding executive office within the company.

The general practice is to adopt or incorporate Article 70 of Table A without amendment. This approach is not, however, without difficulties particularly where the interests of the members of a company and its directors may not coincide. Assume, for example that a company has been incorporated by three individuals A, B and C. A and B are to be engaged as directors of the company and are each to hold 20 per cent of the issued share capital of the company. C does not wish to be a director of the company but has agreed to invest funds in the company in return for the remaining 60 per cent of the issued share capital. The company has adopted Table A for its Articles of Association and, in particular, Article 70 thereof.

Despite his majority shareholding C has, by passing the management of the affairs of the company to the directors, A and B, divested himself of the day-to-day control of the company. Should a dispute now arise between the directors, A and B, and C, the majority shareholder, C may, in practice, have difficulty in exercising control over the directors. The directors may, for example, propose that they enter into service contracts with the company providing for lucrative salaries for a period of five years. They may decide that no dividend should be paid on the ordinary share capital of the company thereby depriving C of any return on his investment. Likewise, they may propose that the company enters into one or more contracts to which, for whatever reason, C is opposed. If the directors have already given effect to such decisions then there will be little or nothing that C can do other than to remove the directors by ordinary resolution. Even this, as we will see, cannot be done immediately. Alternatively, he may be able to raise court proceedings under section 459 of the Companies Act 1985 alleging that the affairs of the company are or have been conducted in a manner which is unfairly prejudicial to himself as a member of the company. He may even wish to seek the winding-up of the company under section 122 of the Insolvency Act 1986. Each of these remedies is however draconian in nature and may result in further loss to C.

To avoid this situation arising it is again necessary to consider incorporating additional provisions within the Articles of Association of a company qualifying Article 70 of Table A or retaining control for the members of the company in respect of particular matters. As previously noted this will be particularly important where the members and directors of the company are not the same individuals.

Borrowing powers of directors

3.3.14 Prior to the introduction of the current Table A, the statutory Table A granted authority to the directors of the company to exercise all the powers of the company to borrow money and to grant security in respect thereof. The standard provision which was contained in Article 79 of the Table A annexed to the Companies Act 1948 contained a restriction upon this authority whereby the amount which the directors were entitled to borrow could not at any time without prior sanction of the company in general meeting exceed the nominal amount of the issued share capital of the company. The general practice was to delete this restriction so that the directors were enabled to exercise all the powers of the company to borrow money and to grant securities. The current Table A does not contain any specific reference to the power of directors to borrow money. Arguably, this power is adequately conferred in terms of Article 70 of the current Table A. It is generally felt, however, that these powers are too important to be left without specific provision and accordingly it is common to incorporate a further article, in addition to Article 70, expressly conferring these powers on the directors of a company. One style for such an article may be found in Article 16 of the amended Articles of Association contained in Schedule 8. Generally, banks and other lending institutions will wish to see such an Article expressly contained within the Articles of Association of a company prior to their advancing funds to the company. This practice is likely to continue notwithstanding the terms of the Companies Act 1989 considered above.

Further provisions regarding directors — Articles 73–98 of Table A

3.3.15 The Articles noted above should be carefully examined by all those involved in limited companies and, in particular, by company directors. Many of these Articles will be discussed in more detail later but, in the meantime, the following points may be made.

(a) Articles 73–75 provide for the retirement of directors by rotation. Unless these articles are excluded or amended, all the directors of a company require to retire from office at the first Annual General Meeting of the company and, if they wish, may thereafter offer themselves for re-election. At each subsequent Annual General Meeting one-third of the directors require to retire from office and again, if they wish, may offer themselves for re-election. These provisions are generally viewed as inappropriate in a small private company and accordingly are frequently excluded from operation.

(b) Article 88 of Table A again provides for the chairman of the company to have a second or casting vote. As noted above this provision should be removed where it would jeopardise the balance between two members or groups of members holding an equal stake in the share capital of the company.

(c) Articles 94–98 of Table A contain provision for the voting of directors on matters in which they are directly and personally interested. In the case of small private companies where the directors and members are the same individuals these restrictions are generally viewed as inappropriate and accordingly it is common to either exclude or amend these provisions. In terms of the amended Articles of Association contained in Schedule 8, Articles 95 and 96 are excluded and an additional Article (No. 20 of the amended Articles) is introduced to enable directors to vote on matters in which they are personally interested. Again care will require to be taken with regard to these Articles where the interests of the members and the directors of a company do not directly coincide.

Company secretary, administration and miscellaneous matters — Articles 99–118 of Table A

The remainder of Table A is devoted to a number of miscellaneous 3.3.16
matters including provision for the company secretary, the keeping of minutes, the use of the company seal, the declaration of dividends, the maintenance of accounts and the capitalisation of profits, the issuing of notices and provisions regarding the winding-up of the company and the indemnification of directors. Generally these are adopted with either no or only minor amendments. The only matter of which mention will be made here relates to the extension of the indemnity granted to directors in terms of Article 118 of Table A. It is common for this limited indemnity to be extended in order to afford the maximum protection to the directors of the company. Any such extension must, however, be read subject to the provisions of section 310 of the Companies Act 1985. This section renders void any exemption or indemnification for the liability of any officer of the company or any person employed as an auditor except in so far as such provision provides for the indemnification of such officer or auditor against any liability incurred in defending proceedings in which judgment is given in his favour or he is acquitted or proceedings under sections 144 or 727 of the 1985 Act in which relief is granted to him by the court. In terms of section 137 of the 1989 Act, section 310 was amended in order to enable companies to obtain directors' and

officers' liability insurance cover. If such cover is taken out, its existence must be disclosed in the annual directors report.

Incorporation Forms and Procedure

3.4 Following the preparation of the Memorandum and Articles of Association, the next step in incorporation is the preparation, signing and submission of these documents together with the required incorporation forms. For a company limited by shares or guarantee, the normal items submitted to the Registrar of Companies for incorporation are as follows:

(a) Memorandum of Association;
(b) Articles of Association;
(c) Companies Forms 10 and 12; and
(d) Dues of Incorporation.

As previously noted both the Memorandum and Articles of Association require to be subscribed by one or more subscribers in the presence of a single witness. The full name, designation and address of each subscriber and of the witness should be carefully typed under their respective signatures. On the Memorandum of Association there should be written alongside the name of each subscriber the number of shares for which he wishes to subscribe. Normally this will be one share only in which case this may be typed alongside the subscriber's name. Both the Memorandum and Articles should contain a note of the date and place of signing. The style Memorandum contained in Schedule 4 gives the preferred format for the execution of the Memorandum of Association; the same form should be followed in the case of the Articles.

Statement of first directors and secretary and intended situation of registered office — Companies Form 10

3.4.1 This form contains the principal information required by the Registrar regarding the first directors, secretary and registered office of the company which it is proposed to incorporate. As with all companies forms this will require to be completed with care and the following points may be worth noting:

(i) *Name of company.* The name of the company should be typed in block capitals. It is essential that the name is identical on all forms submitted and on the Memorandum and Articles of Association;
(ii) *Registered office.* The full postal address of the registered office of the company should be stated including, if available, the post-code;
(iii) *Forms submitted by agents.* Where, as is usual, the forms are submitted by an agent for the subscribers to the Memorandum

and Articles of Association that fact should be noted by marking the box on the front of the form and by giving the full name and address of the agent in question. This information should be duplicated at the foot of the form in the space headed presenter's name, address and reference. This box should be completed identically on all forms submitted;

(iv) *Continuation sheets.* Where it is intended to appoint more than two directors, continuation sheets will be required and the number of continuation sheets should be noted on the front of Form 10;

(v) *Particulars of directors.* Detailed particulars require to be given regarding each of the persons who are to be the first directors of the company. Where the individual in question has no previous names or no other directorships, this fact should be made clear by completing the form with the word "None" where appropriate;

(vi) *Address.* The address given for each director should be his usual residential address;

(vii) *Other directorships.* Each director should disclose all directorships held by him at the time of signing or during the preceding five years. A present or past directorship need not be disclosed if the company in question has been a dormant company throughout the preceding five years in terms of section 250 of the Companies Act 1985 (as inserted by section 14 of the Companies Act 1989);

(viii) *Secretary.* In the case of the company secretary, only his name, any previous name and the usual residential address should be given. Clearly if a firm or company is to be appointed secretary then a business address will be appropriate.

Form 10 requires to be subscribed by each person who is to be a director of the company on incorporation and by the secretary. In addition it should be signed where indicated on the third page either by an agent acting on behalf of the subscribers to the Memorandum and Articles of Association or by all of the subscribers.

Statutory declaration of compliance — Companies Form 12

In terms of section 12 of the Companies Act 1985, the Registrar of Companies may, in deciding whether or not it is appropriate to incorporate a company, rely upon a statutory declaration in the prescribed form. This is to be signed by either a solicitor engaged in the formation of a company or a person named as a director or secretary in Form 10 and states that the requirements of the Companies Act 1985 in respect of registration and of matters precedent and incidental to it have been complied with by the company. Companies Form 12 requires to be submitted in this regard. Again the name of the company should be carefully completed in block capitals and the full name and address of the parties subscribing should be inserted where indicated. That part of the narrative which 3.4.2

is inappropriate should be deleted. Once again the presenter's name, address and reference should be completed giving the place and date of signing. It is generally sufficient to state the town within which the form was subscribed. The form should be signed in the presence of a Notary Public, Justice of the Peace, or in England, a solicitor who should also sign the form where indicated.

General points regarding completion of forms

3.4.3 In the completion of the foregoing forms and in completing any of the other companies forms for submission to the Registrar of Companies, the following general points should be noted.

(a) As a general point of style all forms should be typewritten or, where this is impracticable, should be completed in black ink and in block capitals. In terms of section 706 of the Companies Act 1985 (as amended by section 125 of the 1989 Act) the Registrar can make regulations regarding the format of documents submitted to him for registration.

(b) Where part of a form is inapplicable or where there is no relevant information to be disclosed, this fact should be made clear either by deletion of the appropriate part of the form or by inserting the words "None" or "Not applicable" as appropriate.

(c) On incorporation the company will be allocated a registered number which will appear on the Certificate of Incorporation. This number remains the same throughout the company's life and will not be affected by any change in the company's structure or by a change in the name of the company. It is, accordingly, the best means of identifying a company and requires to be given on any form submitted to the Registrar of Companies following incorporation. It should also, where possible, be quoted in all correspondence with the Registrar. Section 705 of the 1985 Act (amended by Schedule 19 of the 1989 Act) provides that the Registrar may adopt new forms of registered number if this is thought necessary. In the event of a company being asked to change its number under any new scheme, a period of three years will be given to implement the change.

(d) At least one copy of each form submitted to the Registrar of Companies should be retained for lodging with the company books. All forms submitted are retained by the Registrar and accordingly it is important to retain copies in order that a complete record of the affairs of the company can be maintained by the company itself.

(e) For the incorporation forms it is perhaps simpler for all forms to be dated of even date. Where this is not possible care should be taken to ensure that Form 12 postdates the signing of all other forms.

Procedure for incorporation

3.4.4 As stated above the completed forms together with the Memorandum and Articles of Association should be submitted to the Registrar of Companies with an appropriate covering letter. The dues of incorporation (currently £20 in the ordinary case) should also be submitted with the incorporation forms. The cheque should be made payable to the Registrar of Companies. As indicated previously it may be necessary to submit to the Registrar a formal letter of consent from an appropriate body authorising the use of one or more words within the name of the company. Again any such authorisation should be submitted with the incorporation papers and a copy should be retained for the company's own records. If it is intended that the accounting reference date of the company should be other than the last day of the month in which the anniversary of incorporation falls then Companies Form 225 should also be submitted to the Registrar either with the incorporation papers or within nine months of incorporation. This will be dealt with in more detail later.

Same day incorporation and change of name

3.4.5 In the last few years the Registrar of Companies has introduced more streamlined internal arrangements in relation to company incorporations and changes of name. The result has been not only a reduction in the costs of both incorporation and changing a company's name but also the introduction of an expedited same day service for both matters. The cost involved in each case is £100 compared with the usual £20 for incorporation and £10 for a change of name. This service can be extremely useful with the relevant certificate being collectable on the day that the relevant document is lodged provided that this is with Companies House before 3.30 in the afternoon.

Chapter 4

COMMENCING BUSINESS

Certificate of Incorporation

4.1 Following the submission of the Memorandum and Articles of Association, Incorporation Forms and Dues of Incorporation to the Registrar of Companies, there will be a delay of approximately one week prior to the issue by the Registrar of the company's Certificate of Incorporation (unless, of course, the same day incorporation procedure is followed). The issue of the Certificate of Incorporation is conclusive evidence that the requirements of the Companies Act 1985 in respect of registration and related matters have been complied with and that the company has been duly registered in terms of the Act. Accordingly, the Certificate of Incorporation supersedes the prior incorporation forms. Copies of these forms should however be retained in order to complete the company's own records.

The Certificate of Incorporation will give the full registered name of the company including, where appropriate, the word "Limited." It will also specify the registered number of the company and the country in which it has been registered. In the event of the company changing its name the Registrar will issue a Certificate of Incorporation on Change of Name. The registered number of the company will however remain the same until the company is wound up or struck from the Register. Accordingly, the company's registered number is, in many ways, the surest means of identification.

In the unlikely event of an error being made in the Certificate of Incorporation, it should immediately be returned to the Registrar for rectification. The Certificate of Incorporation should be lodged with the remainder of the company's records. In the event of its being lost, damaged or destroyed, a replacement certificate can be obtained from the Registrar on payment of a small fee (currently £6.00 for a copy and £15.00 for a certified copy). If required for exhibition overseas the Registrar will issue a signed duplicate, otherwise a stamped copy will be issued.

Statutory Books

In terms of the Companies Act 1985, every company requires to maintain a number of statutory registers. These should be made up immediately following the incorporation of the company and should be carefully maintained throughout the company's existence. In addition to the registers strictly required by statute, it is common to maintain a number of additional registers which are generally thought to be useful in maintaining an accurate record of the company's affairs. It is possible to purchase a *pro forma* set of "company books" (sometimes referred to as a company kit) from any good law stationer. These are normally produced in a ring binder and, in addition to the statutory and conventional registers, will generally contain *pro forma* minutes for company meetings and share certificates for issue by the company. As an alternative to acquiring ready-made statutory books, it is possible to make up and maintain the required registers using a number of *pro forma* styles kept together in a looseleaf binder. Styles for the principal registers noted below are contained in Schedule 10. 4.2

Register of members

In terms of section 352 of the Companies Act 1985, every company is required to keep a register of its members. In terms of section 22 of the Act, the subscribers of a company's Memorandum are deemed to have agreed to become members of the company and, following the company's incorporation, are to be entered as such in its Register of Members. In addition, every other person who agrees to become a member of the company and whose name is entered in its Register of Members is a member of the company. 4.2.1

In terms of the statutory provisions, the company is required to register the full name and address of every member, the date on which each person was registered as a member and the date on which any person ceased to be a member. In the case of a company having a share capital, the number and class of shares held by each member, together with the amount paid or agreed to be considered as paid on such shares, should be carefully noted. The information regarding the members of a company requires to be retained for a period of 20 years following a person's ceasing to be a member of the company.

The Register of Members is to be retained at the registered office of the company or at such other office where the making up of the register is carried on. The Register of Members of a company registered in England and Wales must however, always be retained in England and Wales and similarly for companies registered in Scotland whose Register of Members must be retained there. If the Register of Members is kept at any place other than its registered office, intimation of that fact requires to be made to the Registrar of Companies on Companies Form 353.

If there are more than 50 members the register must either include a separate index of members or must, in itself, be in such form as to constitute an index. The register and any index is to be available for inspection by any member of the company without charge and by any other person on payment of a prescribed fee. If requested, the company is obliged to provide copies of the whole or any part of the register again on payment of a prescribed fee. In terms of section 723A of the Companies Act 1985 which was introduced by section 143 of the 1989 Act, the Secretary of State has made provision in the Companies (Inspection and Copying of Registers, Indices and Documents) Regulations 1991 (S.I. 1991 No. 1998) relating to rights of inspection and for obtaining copies of any register, index or document kept under the Act including the fees payable. A company may, on giving notice by advertisement in a newspaper circulating in the area in which the company's registered office is situated, close its Register of Members for any period not exceeding 30 days in each year. In practice, this power is rarely exercised although it may be useful for larger companies.

In terms of section 359 of the Companies Act 1985, the court is empowered to order rectification of a company's Register of Members where either the name of any person is, without sufficient cause, entered in or omitted from the register or where default is made or an unnecessary delay takes place in entering on the register the fact of any person having ceased to be a member.

Register of directors

4.2.2 In terms of section 288 of the Companies Act 1985, every company is required to keep at its registered office a register of its directors and secretaries containing prescribed particulars regarding each director and secretary in terms of the Act. Any change in a company's directors or secretary or in regard to the particulars contained in the register must be intimated to the Registrar within 14 days on Companies Forms 288a and b. Again the register is to be available for inspection by any member of the company without charge and by any other person on payment of a prescribed fee in accordance with the Companies (Inspection and Copying of Registers, Indices and Documents) Regulations 1991. In addition to formally appointed directors, the register must also contain details regarding shadow directors which are defined in terms of section 741 of the Act as being any person in accordance with whose directions or instructions the directors of a company are accustomed to act (there being excluded those giving advice in a professional capacity only).

In the case of a director who is an individual the register must disclose:

(a) his or her present christian name and surname;
(b) any former christian name or surname;
(c) his or her usual residential address;
(d) his or her nationality;
(c) his or her business occupation (if any);
(f) particulars of any other directorships held by the director or which have been held by him or her; and
(g) the date of birth of the director.

In the case of a director which is a corporation or a Scottish firm, the register must disclose its corporate or firm name and its registered or principal office.

It is unnecessary for a married woman to disclose her maiden name. With regard to other directorships it is not necessary to disclose these where the directorship ceased more than five years previously or where the company in question is, and has for the previous five years or since its incorporation been, a dormant company in terms of section 250 of the Act.

With regard to the company secretary it is necessary to disclose only:

(a) in the case of an individual, his or her present christian name and surname and any former christian name or surname and his or her usual residential address; and
(b) in the case of a corporation or a Scottish firm its corporate or firm name and its registered or principal office.

Companies Form 288a, which is used to intimate any change in the directors or secretary of a company or in the particulars noted in the register, also operates in the case of appointment as a form of consent which requires to be signed by any person wishing to take up the position of a director or secretary. Although not appearing in the Act, the Registrar has in the past taken the view that the signature of the consenting director or secretary should either be of even date with, or should post date, the date of the meeting at which the appointment was made. The resignation of directors should be intimated on Companies Form 288b. In this case the signature of the retiring director or secretary is not required but it is recommended that a separate letter of resignation be obtained for retention by the company.

Register of directors' interests in shares or debentures

In addition to the register of directors every company is required, 4.2.3
in terms of section 325 of the Companies Act 1985, to maintain a register of directors' interests in shares or debentures of the company. In terms of section 324 of the Act a director is required to intimate to the company in writing any interests he may have in the shares or

debentures of the company including the number and class of shares concerned and any change in that interest. Schedule 13 of the Act contains details regarding the definition of "interest" in terms of the statutory provisions. This includes, in particular, options on shares, shares held by a company in which a director has a controlling interest, certain trust holdings and shares held by a spouse or infant child.

Intimation requires to be made to the company prior to the expiration of five days beginning on the day following that on which the person concerned becomes a director of the company or on which the existence of the interest comes to his knowledge. The statutory provisions including, in particular, Schedule 13 should be carefully examined in any doubtful case.

Following the notification of an interest in terms of section 324 of the Act the company must enter that interest in the register maintained in terms of section 325 of the Act. Once again the statutory provisions apply equally to shadow directors. The register should be kept with the Register of Members and Schedule 13 of the Act again contains provision for its inspection and for the obtaining of copies.

In the case of public companies listed on a recognised investment exchange such as the London Stock Exchange, section 329 of the Act contains additional requirements regarding the intimation of any interest to the London Stock Exchange before the end of the day next following that on which intimation is made to the company, there being disregarded weekends and bank holidays.

Register of certain interests in shares

4.2.4 In terms of section 211 of the Companies Act 1985, every public company is required to maintain a register of certain interests in its shares notified to it in terms of sections 198–202 of the Act. Broadly these relate to any interests held either individually or as part of a group exceeding three per cent of the issued share capital of the company. The register must be made up within three days following the date of intimation which must be given within two days of the relevant event, and the register requires to be kept with the register of members and the register of directors' interests. Again provision is made for the inspection of the register.

Registers of Charges

4.2.5 Part XII of the Companies Act 1985 (as amended by Part IV of the 1989 Act) contains detailed provisions regarding the registration of certain charges created by a company whether registered in England and Wales or in Scotland. A charge is defined as being any form of security interest (fixed or floating) over property other than an interest arising by operation of law. The Act then states which charges are to be registrable. The definition of a registrable charge has caused some difficulty in the past. It includes, however, a floating charge and any mortgage or standard security granted by the company. In addition to registration in the public Register of Charges, every company requires, in terms of section 411 of the Act, to maintain a Register of Charges granted by it. The register is to be kept at the registered office of the company and is to contain brief details of any charge granted including a short description of the property charged, the amount of the charge and the person entitled to it. A copy of each charge granted is also to be retained by the company. It is common for companies to register the granting of a number of documents such as guarantees and letters of offset even although these may not technically constitute charges in terms of the statutory provisions. In cases of doubt however, it is always prudent to comply with the statutory requirements even although these may not be strictly applicable.

Conventional registers

In addition to the foregoing statutory registers, it is common for companies to maintain a number of additional registers simply as a matter of convenience. These may include any one or more of the following: 4.2.6

(a) a register of allotments giving details of any shares issued by the company;
(b) a register of transfers giving details of any transfers of shares by the members of the company; and
(c) a register of all documents formally executed by the company.

In the case of small private companies it is common also for the minutes of board and company meetings to be maintained as part of the company books. Where this is impracticable however, a separate minute book should be maintained in terms of section 382 of the Companies Act 1985. In terms of this section, every company requires to maintain minutes of all meetings of its members or directors. Minutes should be signed by the chairman of the meeting in question or of the next meeting, following which they are deemed to be "evidence of the proceedings" of the meeting. In terms of section 382(A) of the 1985 Act which was inserted by section 113 of the 1989 Act, a record of written resolutions is also to be maintained. In this case, however, the record may be signed by any director or by the company secretary. In terms of section 383 of the Act, the minutes of any general meeting are to be kept at the company's registered office and are to be available for inspection by any member of the company. Again, the Secretary of State has made detailed provision for inspection in terms of the Companies (Inspection and Copying of Registers, Indices, and Documents) Regulations 1991.

It is also useful to maintain with the company books an up-to-date print of the Memorandum and Articles of Association of the company, the Certificate of Incorporation and any Certificate of Incorporation on Change of Name, copies of all forms submitted to the Registrar of Companies including the incorporation forms and any other miscellaneous documents relating to the affairs of the company including stock transfer forms, notices of meetings and the like.

Company Seal

4.3 It used to be a requirement that every company had a company seal for the formal sealing of documents. The need for a seal was dispensed with by the Requirements of Writing (Scotland) Act 1995. Nevertheless companies can continue to use a seal if they so choose although it is hard to imagine what purpose this now serves. If wished a company seal can be ordered from law stationers. Generally this will either be a pliers seal or a lever press seal. The lever press seal is slightly more expensive but is generally to be preferred. In terms of section 350 of the Companies Act 1985, where a company has a seal this should have engraved upon it in legible characters the full name of the company. The seal should be kept in a secure place available for the execution of formal deeds by the company. Generally the seal is the responsibility of the company secretary. While it is generally inadvisable for a company to have more than one seal, this is permitted by the Act where a company operates in a number of countries (see section 39 of the Act) or where a company maintains a separate seal for sealing share certificates in terms of section 40 of the Act.

Execution of Documents

4.4.1 It may be useful to add here a note regarding the execution and signing of company documents. Section 130 of the Companies Act 1989 replaced the previous provisions of section 36 of the 1985 Act adding three further sections numbered respectively 36A, B and C. Taking account of further changes introduced by the Requirements of Writing (Scotland) Act 1995, these statutory provisions may be summarised as follows.

(a) Dealing firstly with English law, the Act states that a document is executed by a company by the affixing of the common seal of the company. A company need not however now have a common seal and a document may equally be executed by being signed by a director and the secretary of the company or by any two directors where it is expressed, in whatever form of words, to be executed by the company in which case the document is to be treated as if executed under the common seal of the company.

(b) A document which makes it clear on its face that it is intended to be a deed (giving that word its technical English meaning) shall have effect, upon delivery, as a deed and shall be presumed to be delivered, unless a contrary intention is shown, on execution.

(c) Particular provision is made in England and Wales for the benefit of a purchaser from a company in good faith and for valuable consideration where it is stated that a document shall be deemed, in favour of such a purchaser, to have been duly executed by the company if it purports to be signed by a director and the secretary or by any two directors.

(d) In Scotland a document may be signed by a company by being signed on its behalf by a single director or by the secretary or by a person authorised to sign the document on behalf of the company. A document is to be presumed to have been subscribed by a company in accordance with the foregoing provision if it bears to have been subscribed on behalf of the company by a director, the secretary or a person authorised to subscribe the document on the company's behalf and it bears to have been signed by a person as a witness to the subscription of the director, secretary or other person. Alternatively the document will be presumed to have been properly signed if it is signed by two directors or by one director and the secretary or by two authorised persons.

(e) It is expressly stated that a company need not now have a company seal.

These lamentable provisions marked a clear change in the Scottish law with regard to the execution of company documents. The differing provisions applying north and south of the Border are to be regretted and benefit no one other than lawyers. This is further complicated by the provision in section 41 of the 1985 Act that documents may be authenticated under the law of England and Wales by the signature of a director, the company secretary or any authorised officer of the company. This section should not be relied upon north of the Border. Where a Company has adopted Article 101 of Table A or an article in similar terms then if a deed is sealed two directors or one director and the company secretary will require to sign the deed. 4.4.2

Section 38 of the Act gives express authority for a company to appoint an attorney under the law of England and Wales to execute deeds abroad on behalf of the company. It might be assumed from this express authority that, by implication, it is not possible for companies to appoint an attorney to execute deeds in the United Kingdom or for that matter for an attorney to be appointed under Scots Law, the section being stated not to extend to Scotland. In the past, generally, this interpretation has not been accepted and it has 4.4.3

been common for companies, particularly building companies, to appoint attorneys to execute deeds on their behalf. It is likely that, notwithstanding the rather unhelpful terms of the Act, attorneys will continue to be appointed in Scotland also. When accepting such a deed, a copy of the Power of Attorney should be retained with the deed for reference purposes.

As stated, companies may also authorise individuals other than their directors or secretary to sign deeds on their behalf. This is particularly common in the case of a depute or assistant secretary. In any such case, a copy of the relevant Board Minute or other authority should again be obtained for retention with the deed.

Company Stationery and Identification

4.5 The Companies Act 1985 contains a number of provisions regarding the identification and disclosure of certain information by companies. As we have seen this is a direct corollary of the limited liability enjoyed by the majority of companies.

In terms of section 348 of the Companies Act 1985, every company requires to paint or affix its name on the outside of every office or place in which its business is carried on, including its registered office. Likewise the company's full name is to be disclosed in legible characters on all business letters, notices and other official publications of the company and on all invoices, cheques and other bills of exchange or the like. As noted previously it is particularly important that the full name of the company (including the word "Limited" where appropriate) is used on all cheques issued by the company. As we have seen, any officer of a company who signs a cheque on behalf of a company in which the company's full name is not mentioned is liable not only to a fine but may also be personally liable to the holder of the cheque unless this is duly paid by the company.

In addition to the name of the company, a company requires to disclose on all business letters and order forms the following additional information:

(a) the country of registration and the company's registered number;
(b) the registered office of the company;
(c) in the case of an investment company as defined by section 266 of the Act the fact that it is such a company; and
(d) in the case of a limited company exempt from the obligation to use the word "Limited" as part of its name the fact that it is a limited company.

Any reference to share capital on company stationery must be to the paid up share capital of the company. This is intended to prevent misleading statements as to the value of a company's share capital. Again where reference is made to one or more of the directors of a company, the names of all directors must be disclosed (this does not apply in the case of a director's name being added merely as signatory to letters on behalf of a company). It is suggested that directors' names be omitted from company stationery to avoid unnecessary cost when changes occur.

Miscellaneous Matters

A number of additional items are commonly dealt with immediately following incorporation. These will generally include the following. 4.6

Company bank accounts

It is important that, from the date of its incorporation, all payments made or received by the company be transacted through the company's own bank account(s). As with an individual, a company can open a number of different forms of account the most common being current and deposit accounts. In the case of a company however, the bank will normally require a completed minute of a meeting of the company authorising the directors to open such accounts as may be required and granting the necessary authority to one or more individuals to sign cheques on behalf of the company. In addition, the banks will generally require a copy of the Memorandum and Articles of Association of the company and a copy of the Certificate of Incorporation and any Certificate of Incorporation on Change of Name. 4.6.1

There are a number of possibilities for the method of a company drawing cheques and this is clearly a matter for decision by the individuals concerned. There may be obvious risks in enabling a single individual to authorise and sign cheques on the company's behalf and, with this in mind, many companies choose to require two signatories to each cheque. Alternatively, the bank may be authorised to accept cheques with only one signature up to a specified level above which two signatories are again required. The bank will require specimen signatures of all parties authorised to sign cheques on the company's behalf. It is worth pointing out that authorised signatories need not necessarily be directors of the company or the company secretary.

Memorandum and Articles of Association

As discussed at length in Chapter 3, the Memorandum and Articles of Association are the founding documents of the company and are essential in regulating the relationship between the members and directors of the company and between the company itself and the world at large. It is recommended therefore that, immediately following incorporation, the directors of the company be provided 4.6.2

with a copy of the Memorandum and Articles of Association for their own information and retention. Likewise where a company is incorporated with only a handful of members, it may be useful to provide each member with a copy of the Memorandum and Articles.

Registration for value added tax (VAT)

4.6.3 A company will become liable to register for VAT when it considers that there are good grounds for believing that the value of its taxable supplies will exceed £48,000 (the current turnover threshold) within the next 30 days, or if the value of its taxable supplies in the previous 12 months has exceeded that threshold. The relevant VAT form (VAT 1) should be completed and submitted to the local office of H.M. Customs and Excise which will, in due course, advise the company of its registration number. This number should then be incorporated on all invoices, order forms and the like. The company may also have to consider registration under other legislation such as the Consumer Credit Act, the Financial Services Act or the Data Protection Act. Separate advice should be sought on all such matters where appropriate.

Registration for charitable purposes

4.6.4 Where a company wishes to be treated as a charitable company for tax purposes the procedures to be followed vary north and south of the Border. To deal with these in turn.

(a) In England the company must apply to the Charity Commissioners for registration as a charity in terms of the Charities Act 1993. The company must comply with the requirements relating to charities contained within the Act. Application is made by submission of a copy of the Memorandum and Articles of Association of the Company, together with a copy of the Certificate of Incorporation and any Certificate of Incorporation on Change of Name to the Charity Commission, St Albans House, 57/60 Haymarket, London SW1.

(b) In Scotland the company must apply to the Inland Revenue claims branch at Trinity Park House, South Trinity Road, Edinburgh for registration for charitable purposes. Application is made by submitting a copy of the Memorandum and Articles of Association of the company together with a copy of the Certificate of Incorporation. It is important to request that the Revenue confirm that the company will be treated as charitable from the date of incorporation. The Revenue will, in due course, issue a determination, a copy of which should be lodged with the company books. If accepted for charitable purposes, a copy of the annual accounts of the company should, in each year, be forwarded to the Inland Revenue claims branch for their perusal.

It is important to note that the acceptance of a company's charitable status in Scotland is provided for in terms of section 505 of the Income and Corporation Taxes Act 1988. The English law relating to the registration of charities and the charities commission does not extend to Scotland.

In all but the most straightforward cases it may be worthwhile submitting draft documentation to the Inland Revenue for comment prior to the company papers being forwarded to the Registrar of Companies for incorporation. This may avoid needless changes at a later date.

Public company's trading certificate

Where a company has been incorporated as a public company it is prohibited from commencing business or from borrowing any money until it has obtained a certificate from the Registrar of Companies in terms of section 117 of the Companies Act 1985. The Registrar issues the statutory certificate only once he has been satisfied that the nominal value of the company's allotted share capital is not less than the authorised minimum, currently £50,000. In order to obtain a trading certificate, as it is commonly known, the company must submit a statutory declaration in the prescribed form confirming the nominal and paid-up capital of the company and detailing any preliminary expenses or payments made to promoters of the company. At least one quarter of the nominal value and the whole of any premium on shares issued must have been paid up. 4.6.5

Corporation tax

Following incorporation, a company will receive its first tax form from H.M. Inspector of Taxes. This form (CT41G) is required by the Inland Revenue to give basic details regarding the company for tax record purposes. Details include the address of the company's accountants, its accounting reference date and details regarding the directors of the company including, in particular, their national insurance numbers. The form requires to be completed and returned to the local tax office along with a copy of the Memorandum and Articles of Association of the company if required by the Inland Revenue. 4.6.6

Company Borrowing and Securities

Frequently one of the first acts of a company will be to raise funds by borrowing money. A company can of course also raise funds by issuing shares. In the case of small private companies however, it may be difficult to find a buyer for the company's shares and the promoters 4.7

of the company itself may themselves have limited funds to invest in the enterprise. As a result companies frequently turn to raising loan capital as opposed to equity. Loan capital also has some other characteristics which may make it more attractive than issuing shares. Generally speaking loans will bear interest at a fixed rate or at a rate fluctuating with bank lending rates. As a result even although the company is extremely successful it will continue to pay the same rate to its creditor. On the other hand of course interest to creditors requires to be paid even although a company is not performing as well as might be hoped. This problem does not ordinarily arise in the case of share capital where dividends can only be paid from distributable profits. Interest paid by a company on loans can however generally be set against the profits of the company for tax purposes. This does not apply in the case of dividends paid on the share capital of the company which instead give rise to a requirement to pay advance corporation tax, literally a payment to account of tax, on the amount of the dividend. Although advance corporation tax paid can then be set against any corporation tax liability of the company, this is dependent on the company realising profits on which tax is to be paid. There will also be some delay in the company recovering the tax paid. Finally, and again where the company is successful, the raising of capital by way of loan avoids watering down the promoters' share of the equity of the company by issuing further shares. Generally companies seek to have a balance between share and loan capital. Indeed lenders will ordinarily look to ensure that a company's "gearing" (as the ratio between equity and loan capital is commonly referred to) is acceptable to the lender. The lender will wish to see that the company has a suitable balance between the two types of capital.

Few lenders will advance funds to a company without some form of security being given either by the company itself or, where a company has insufficient funds, by those involved with the company. As we have considered already, company shareholders and directors should seek to avoid giving personal securities for the indebtedness of the company if this is at all possible. It is suggested that it is preferable, where possible, for promoters to invest sufficient capital in the company itself thereby providing the company with funds which may either reduce the requirement for borrowings or give some security to the lender rather than the promoter giving personal guarantees or securities. Assuming that the company is in a position to give some security this may be dealt with in exactly the same manner as a security would be granted by an individual. The principal exception, as we have seen, is in relation to the granting of a floating charge which is a form of security available to companies alone. Generally lenders will instruct solicitors to deal with the preparation of the required security documentation. Alternatively this will be dealt with by the lender itself. The key point to note in relation to all such securities is that, in order to be effective, any charge granted by a company must be registered with the Registrar of Companies within 21 days of its creation. Detailed provisions in this regard are contained within Part IV of the Companies Act 1989 although these have not yet replaced the existing provisions in sections 395 and following of the Companies Act 1985. Generally, failure to register a charge within the 21-day period renders it unenforceable against a liquidator, administrator or any subsequent purchaser of the property. There is provision for late registration but this will only be effective prior to any insolvency and where it can be shown that the company was solvent at the relevant time. Clearly therefore the registration of charges within the public register is essential from the point of view of the lender and, as a result, it is generally the lender or his agent who deals with registration. The responsibility does however rest with the company itself and failure to deliver particulars of the charge within the 21-day period is an offence. As we have seen, the company is also responsible for the registration of any charge granted in the company's own Register of Charges. Although failure in this regard also constitutes an offence it does not affect the validity of the security, unlike failing to register a charge publicly.

CHAPTER 5

COMPANY MEETINGS

5.1 The procedure for and administration of company meetings is regulated not only by the Companies Act 1985 but also, as we have seen, by the Articles of Association of the company. Accordingly both the Act and the company's own Articles of Association must be carefully examined and adhered to in relation to any meetings of the members or directors of the company. In many cases and particularly where a small company is both owned and managed by a few individuals, the formal meetings of the company required by statute or otherwise will not, in fact, take place. Instead the secretary will simply be asked to prepare the necessary documentation calling and minuting the "meeting" in order to give effect of the wishes of the participators. While this device is frequently resorted to, great care should be taken that each of the individuals concerned knows of and agrees with the formal procedure being waived. If the issue in question is at all contentious and is not known to be agreed by all the parties in question, then a formal meeting should always be held and the full statutory procedure and the procedure laid down in the Articles of Association of the company should be strictly adhered to.

Meetings of Members

5.2 The seat of power within any company, in theory at least, lies with its members, even although, as we have seen, the day-to-day management of the company will ordinarily be delegated to the directors of the company. Any major change in the structure of a company or in the direction of its activities will ordinarily require the consent of the members of the company obtained at a general meeting of the company. General meetings fall into two categories; the Annual General Meeting of the company and Extraordinary General Meetings. Every company must hold an Annual General Meeting in each calendar year unless dispensed with by an elective resolution as noted hereafter. The only other exception is that a company need not hold an Annual General Meeting in the year of its incorporation or in the following year provided that the first Annual General Meeting is held within eighteen months of the date of its incorporation. In terms of section 366 of the Companies Act 1985, no more than 15 months must elapse between each Annual General Meeting of the company. As a matter of practice, it is recommended that following the first Annual General Meeting of the company every succeeding Annual General Meeting is held on or about the same time in each year. By this means, the matter largely becomes one of routine and a target date is automatically set for various related matters such as the preparation of accounts and the annual directors' report. All other general meetings are referred to as Extraordinary General Meetings (see Article 36 of Table A).

A number of items are generally dealt with at the Annual General Meeting of a company. These include the approval of the company's accounts including the auditors' and directors' reports, the declaration of a dividend, the election or re-election of directors, the appointment of auditors and giving the directors of the company authority to fix the remuneration of the auditors. Such matters are generally referred to as the ordinary business of the meeting. Any additional business is referred to as special business.

Notice of General Meetings

In terms of section 369 of the Companies Act 1985, an Annual General Meeting requires at least 21 clear days' notice. An Extraordinary General Meeting requires at least 14 clear days' notice unless a special resolution is to be passed in which case at least 21 clear days' notice will be required. Article 38 of Table A reiterates and expands upon the statutory notice requirement and further provisions regarding the notice itself are contained in Articles 111–116 of Table A. These articles are generally adopted without alteration. 5.3

In terms of section 369, it is possible for the members of a company to consent to a meeting being called upon short notice. In the case of an Annual General Meeting, all members entitled to attend and vote at the meeting require to consent, in writing, to its being called upon short notice. In the case of an Extraordinary General Meeting, members having a right to attend and vote and together holding not less than 95 per cent in nominal value of the issued share capital of the company (or in the case of a guarantee company representing not less than 95 per cent of the total voting rights of the company) require to consent if the meeting is to be called upon short notice. As we shall see in paragraph 5.7, this percentage may be adjusted marginally to not less than 90 per cent by an elective resolution. Where a meeting is to be called on short notice a form of consent should be signed by each of the consenting members. Where the company has only a few members, then it may be possible to incorporate this as a simple docquet typed at the foot of the notice calling the meeting 5.3.1

and signed by the members. A style docquet which can also be adapted for use as a separate form of consent forms part of the styles contained in Schedule 14.

5.3.2 Notice of general meetings must be given to all members of the company and to the company's directors and auditors. Article 39 of Table A provides that the accidental failure to give notice to a particular member shall not invalidate the proceedings at a meeting. This provision should only be relied upon in exceptional cases. If a company deliberately fails to serve notice of a meeting upon a particular member, then the proceedings at that meeting may well be invalidated. Notice of all meetings (except board meetings) requires to be given in writing. In addition, in the case of a company having a share capital, every notice must contain a statement that a member entitled to attend and vote is entitled to appoint one or more proxies to attend and, on a poll, to vote instead of him and that a proxy need not be a member of the company (section 372 of the Companies Act 1985). The appointment of proxies will be dealt with later in this chapter.

5.3.3 The notice of a meeting should also clearly and accurately state the business to be transacted at the meeting. Generally no item of business can be transacted unless proper notice has been given. In the case of a resolution to be put to a meeting, a full transcript of the resolution as proposed should be contained within the notice which should also specify the type of resolution required. It is competent (and common) to refer to annexed or identified deeds in the terms of the resolution provided that these are clearly incorporated by reference into the body of the notice. The chairman of a meeting may, in certain circumstances, accept an amendment to a resolution at the meeting itself. He can only do so however, within very limited bounds. Where, for example it is proposed to increase the share capital of the company to say, £100,000, it might be possible for the chairman to accept an amendment to that resolution whereby the share capital would be increased to only £50,000. He could not however, accept an amended resolution increasing the capital to £150,000. The test in each case must be whether or not the amendment proposed might have altered the decision of any member to attend the meeting and vote in favour of or against the resolution in question. In cases of doubt, any amendment should be resisted.

Calling of Meetings

5.4 Meetings can be summoned or requisitioned by a number of individuals and groups. In terms of Article 37 of Table A, the directors are empowered to call general meetings of the company and in the majority of cases notice of meetings will be issued by the secretary of the company on the authority of the board.

In terms of section 368 of the Companies Act 1985, however, the members of a company are also empowered to requisition the company to hold an Extraordinary General Meeting. Members holding not less than one-tenth of the paid-up capital of the company carrying the right to vote at general meetings of the company or, in the case of a company without a share capital, members representing not less than one-tenth of the total voting rights of all members of the company, must lodge a written requisition, signed by the requisitionists and stating the objects of the meeting at the registered office of the company. The requisition may consist of a number of documents in like form, each signed by one or more of the requisitionists. Upon receipt of the requisition, the directors must forthwith convene an Extraordinary General Meeting of the company for the purposes stated in the requisition. Should the directors fail to convene a meeting within 21 days of the date of lodging of the requisition or if they convene a meeting for a date more than 28 days after the date of the notice then the requisitionists, or any of them representing more than one-half of the total voting rights of all of them, may themselves convene a meeting provided that this be held within three months from the date of deposit of the requisition. In this event, the requisitionists may recover any reasonable expenses incurred by them as a result of the directors' failure to requisition a meeting from the company itself and any such sums paid by the company may be deducted from monies due to the directors. 5.4.1

The statutory provision for the requisition of meetings by members is, in practice, rarely exercised. It may however, be a useful device where the directors of a company are acting without regard to the interests of the company's members or a part thereof. In some cases however, it may be simpler to proceed by the alternative route specified in section 370 of the Act whereby any two or more members holding not less than one-tenth of the issued share capital of the company or, if the company does not have a share capital, not less than 5 per cent in number of the members of the company may themselves call a meeting of the company. Clearly this avoids the requisition procedure although the members will not be able to recover their costs from the company.

In certain limited circumstances both the court and the Secretary of State may call a meeting of a company (see sections 367 and 371 of the Companies Act 1985). These provisions are rarely used although the court's power to convene a meeting may be useful where, for whatever reason, the members of a company are themselves unable to call a meeting. In either case, it is open to the Secretary of State or the court to provide that, at any meeting called by them, one person alone may constitute a quorum. The auditor of a company can also convene a meeting of the company in terms of section 392A of the Companies Act 1985 as inserted by section 122 of the 1989 Act. This 5.4.2

arises where a resigning auditor considers that circumstances connected with his resignation should be placed before the members of the company. Finally in this connection, reference is made to section 142 of the Companies Act 1985 in terms of which the directors of a public company are obliged to call an Extraordinary General Meeting of the company if the assets of the company fall below one-half of the value of the called-up share capital of the company. Notice of the meeting must be issued within 28 days of the directors becoming aware of the situation and the meeting itself must be held within 56 days of that date. The meeting is required in order to consider what steps, if any, require to be taken by the company in the circumstances.

Special Notice Procedure

5.5 In certain situations, a company requires to follow a more rigorous procedure in giving notice of its general meetings. The procedure provided for is referred to as special notice procedure and is governed by section 379 of the Companies Act 1985. In terms of the section, 28 days' notice must be given of the intention to make any resolution requiring special notice procedure. In terms of the Act, special notice is required in the following circumstances:

(a) on a resolution to remove a director (section 303 of the Act);
(b) on a resolution appointing a director who exceeds the age limit of 70 for public companies (section 293 of the Act); and
(c) the appointment of an auditor other than the retiring auditor or the removal of an auditor before the expiration of his term of office (section 391A of the Act).

Resolutions

5.6 A number of different types of resolution are provided for in terms of the Companies Act 1985, namely ordinary, extraordinary, special and, following upon section 116 of the 1989 Act, elective resolutions. An ordinary resolution requires a simple majority of members voting at the meeting and requires 14 days' notice. Section 378 of the Act contains provisions regarding extraordinary and special resolutions. Both these types of resolution require a majority of not less than three-fourths of the members voting either in person or by proxy. A special resolution requires 21 days' notice unless, as we have seen, the required majority of members consents to the resolution being put after a shorter period of notice.

Elective Resolutions

5.7 Section 116 of the Companies Act 1989 provided for a new statutory provision to be inserted as section 379A of the 1985 Act. This section deals with the passing of elective resolutions by private companies. An elective resolution is required for the carrying through of certain particular types of business arising from the attempts in the 1989 Act to introduce some deregulation in the affairs of private limited companies.

In order to pass an elective resolution, at least 21 days' notice in writing requires to be given stating that an elective resolution is to be proposed and giving the terms of the resolution. The resolution requires to be approved by all the members entitled to attend and vote at the meeting in question. The terms of an elective resolution may be revoked at any time by the passing of an ordinary resolution to that effect. The resolution also ceases to have effect if the company is re-registered as a public company.

The provisions of the Companies Act which may be dispensed with by the use of an elective resolution are as follows:

(a) The authority of directors to allot relevant securities under section 80 of the Companies Act 1985 may now be granted for an indefinite period or for a fixed period in excess of the former limit of five years.

(b) A private company can now dispense with the requirement to lay annual accounts and reports before a general meeting of the company under section 252 of the 1985 Act as inserted by section 16 of the 1989 Act. Accounts still require to be prepared and circulated to members and any member or the auditors of the company can, by notice to the company, require that the accounts be laid before the company in general meeting.

(c) A private company can now dispense with the requirement to hold an Annual General Meeting. The Act does however provide that any shareholder may require the holding of such a meeting by giving notice to the company not later than three months prior to the end of the year.

(d) The majority required to authorise the calling of an Extraordinary General Meeting on short notice can now be reduced from the former requirement of 95 per cent of shareholders to a lesser percentage being not less than 90 per cent.

(e) A private company can also now elect to dispense with the annual reappointment of auditors in which event the company's auditors shall be deemed to be reappointed for each succeeding financial year so long as the resolution is in force.

(f) Finally, the Secretary of State is authorised, in terms of the Act, to make further provision enabling private companies to dispense with requirements which, in his opinion, relate primarily to the internal administration and procedure of companies.

Written Resolutions

5.8 Section 113 of the 1989 Act introduces a number of new provisions to the 1985 Act numbered respectively sections 381A, 381B, 381C and 382A. In terms of these provisions of the Act, any matter which may be done by a private company by resolution of the company in general meeting (or any class of the members of the company) may now be done without a meeting and without any notice being required by resolution in writing signed by or on behalf of all of the members of the company entitled to attend and vote at such a meeting. All forms of resolution, be they ordinary, special, extraordinary or elective can be passed by this means. This rule is however expressly stated not to apply in the case of a resolution under section 303 of the Act to remove a director prior to the expiration of his period of office or to a resolution under section 391 removing an auditor. A number of procedural requirements are also specified in Schedule 15A to the Companies Act 1985 in relation to certain key matters including the disapplication of pre-emption rights, where financial assistance is given for the purchase of a company's own shares or that of its holding company, the purchase by a company of its own shares, the approval of a director's service contract and the funding of directors' expenditure in performing their duties.

In terms of the Deregulation (Resolutions of Private Companies) Order 1996 (S.I. 1996 No. 1471) which restated section 381B, a copy of all written resolutions is to be passed to the auditors of the company or they are otherwise to be notified of their contents at or before the resolutions being signed by members. It is a criminal offence not to copy written resolutions to the auditors or to advise them of their terms. However failure to comply does not now affect the validity of the resolutions. A record of all written resolutions is to be maintained by the company in the same manner as the minutes of the company are currently maintained. For completeness an acknowledgement should also be obtained from the auditors and a copy kept with the resolutions.

Many companies already provided for the passing of written resolutions in terms of their Articles of Association without any requirement for referral of such resolutions to the auditors of the company. The statutory procedure is in addition to such an arrangement and does not prevent a company relying on the procedure specified in its Articles should it choose to do so. Article 53 of the Articles contained in the current Table A makes express provision in this regard although there remain doubts as to whether this can be used to pass a resolution which is stated by the Companies Acts to require passing at a general meeting of the Company.

Voting Rights

In the absence of any specific rules in the Articles of Association of the company, the voting on a resolution may be either on a show of hands, when each member will normally have a single vote, or on a poll where each member will ordinarily have a single vote for each share held by him. Where a company has issued stock instead of shares then, unless otherwise provided, the member will have one vote for every £10 of stock held. As we shall see, a proxy is not entitled to vote on a show of hands, except in relation to a demand for a poll. In terms of section 373 of the Act, any provision in a company's articles is void if it would have the effect of excluding the right to demand a poll in respect of any matter other than the election of a chairman of the meeting or its adjournment, or if it rendered ineffective a demand for a poll on any such question made either: 5.9

(a) by not less than five members having a right to attend and vote at the meeting; or
(b) by a member or members representing not less than one tenth of the total voting rights of all members having the right to vote at the meeting; or
(c) by a member or members holding shares in the company conferring a right to vote at the meeting being shares on which an aggregate sum has been paid up equal to not less than one tenth of the total sum paid up on all shares conferring that right.

As will be seen from Article 46 of Table A, which is commonly adopted without modification, it is usual to extend the members' rights to demand a poll by giving such a right to any two members having the right to vote at the meeting, and also by giving a similar right to the chairman of the meeting. Indeed, frequently the Articles will provide that any member may demand a poll. In all but the most straightforward cases, it is recommended that, where a poll requires to be held, the chairman adjourn the meeting for a brief period in order to enable simple voting slips to be prepared and issued to members in order that their votes might be carefully and accurately recorded and checked against members' shareholdings in the company's Register of Members. Where there are a number of members present it may be useful to appoint one or more scrutineers to arrange and supervise the taking of a poll. Style documentation in this regard is contained in Schedule 11.

Again it should be stressed that in every case, the Articles of Association of the company should be checked with regard to voting rights and the procedure at meetings. It is by no means unusual for certain shares to carry weighted voting rights, either generally or in relation to specific matters, or for certain classes of shares to be excluded from voting altogether.

Proxies and Corporate Representatives

5.10.1 As we have seen, any member of a company is entitled in terms of section 372 of the Act to appoint a proxy to attend and vote at meetings on his behalf. A proxy need not be a member of the company. This right does not apply in the case of a company not having a share capital unless specifically provided for in the Articles of Association of the company. A member of a private company cannot, unless the Articles so provide, appoint more than one proxy for a specific occasion. Subject to this qualification, the provision for a proxy provides a useful mechanism for a member securing access for another individual (for example his solicitor or accountant) to a meeting. The principal restriction on a proxy is that, in the absence of express provision in the Articles, he is unable to vote on a show of hands except for a show of hands to demand a poll. In the case of a private company, a proxy can speak at the meeting in so far as the member himself would be able to do so. The exact extent of this right is uncertain.

As we have seen, every notice calling a general meeting of the company must include a statement confirming the rights of a member to appoint a proxy to attend and vote on his behalf. Articles 60–62 of Table A contain provisions for the appointment of proxies including styles for the instrument appointing a proxy. In terms of Article 56 of Table A, the instrument appointing a proxy must be deposited at the registered office of the company or at such other office as may be specified in accordance with the Articles for the deposit of instruments of proxy not less than 48 hours before the time appointed for the holding of the meeting in question. This rule, which is generally adopted by companies without qualification, reflects the provision of section 372 whereby any provision in the Articles would be void in so far as it would have the effect of requiring the deposit of an instrument appointing a proxy more than 48 hours before the meeting in question.

5.10.2 A proxy should not be confused with a corporate representative appointed in terms of section 375 of the Act. A corporation (which term includes all limited companies within the meaning of the Act) may appoint a representative to attend and vote at company meetings on its behalf. Any such representative is entitled to exercise the same powers on behalf of the corporation which he represents as that corporation would itself be able to exercise if it were an individual member. A corporate representative is not therefore restricted in the same manner as a proxy and the time-limit for the deposit of instruments of proxy does not apply to a corporate representative. In cases of dispute however, a chairman would be entitled to be satisfied regarding the appointment of the representative appearing at a meeting. Where the matter in question is contentious it is therefore prudent for a corporate representative to be supplied with an excerpt board minute confirming his authority as representative of the corporation.

Quorum

In terms of section 370(4) of the Companies Act 1985, any two members personally present constitute a quorum unless the Articles of Association provide otherwise. Article 40 of Table A provides that any two persons entitled to vote upon the business to be transacted (each being a member or a proxy for a member or a duly authorised representative of a corporation) shall constitute a quorum. Companies may alter the requirements for a quorum and, once again, the Articles of Association of the company should be carefully checked in this regard since, in the absence of a quorum, a meeting is not properly constituted. 5.11

Members' Resolutions

In terms of sections 376 and 377 of the Companies Act 1985, the members of a company may requisition the company in writing requiring the company to give notice of any resolution which it is intended to move at the next annual general meeting of the company and, in addition, to circulate to the members a statement of not more than one thousand words with respect to the matter referred to in any proposed resolution. The logic of restricting this right to Annual General Meetings is uncertain. The number of members necessary for a requisition under this provision is either: 5.12

(i) a number representing not less than one-twentieth of the total voting rights of all the members having, at the date of requisition, a right to vote at the meeting to which the requisition relates; or
(ii) not less than 100 members holding shares in the company on which there has been paid up an average sum for each member of not less than £100.

The statutory provisions contain a detailed procedure to be followed in the case of any such resolution, including provision for the payment of the company's expenses. However a company need not comply with a requisition if satisfied that the statutory procedure is being abused to secure needless publicity for defamatory matters.

Minutes

5.13 Sections 382 and 383 of the Companies Act 1985 contain provisions regarding the maintenance of a record of company meetings. A company is required to keep minutes of the proceedings of all general meetings, board meetings and, where there are managers, managers' meetings. As we have seen in terms of the Act, any such minute, if purporting to be signed by the chairman of the meeting at which the proceedings were held or by the chairman of the next succeeding meeting, "is evidence of the proceedings". It is generally assumed that minutes signed by the chairman are *prima facie* evidence of proceedings but that this presumption may be rebutted by evidence led to the contrary. Minute books are to be kept at a company's registered office and minutes of general meetings are to be available for inspection by any member of the company in accordance with the Companies (Inspection and Copying of Registers, Indices and Documents) Regulations 1991. A member is also entitled to obtain copies of the minutes of any general meeting on payment of a prescribed fee.

The importance of maintaining up-to-date and accurate company minutes cannot be stressed too much. The minutes form an essential part of the history of the company and frequently have to be relied upon in the case of a dispute between the members or directors of the company. The amount of detail recorded will, of course, largely depend upon circumstances. The Schedules contain a number of style minutes relating to various matters. These styles assume that the matter is not contentious in any way and that the members and directors are generally agreed upon the course of action to be followed. Where the matter is one of dispute, a more detailed minute may be appropriate.

Board Meetings

5.14 The statutory provisions relate, in the main, to general meetings of the members of a company. The procedure to be followed in relation to board meetings is generally more informal. For example, written notice may not be required in the case of small companies with only two or three directors. Articles 88–98 of Table A contain detailed provisions regarding the proceedings of directors and these are commonly adopted without alteration. Once again, however, the Articles of Association of each company should be carefully examined in case they contain any provisions peculiar to the company in question.

CHAPTER 6

COMPANY DIRECTORS AND SECRETARIES

Definition of Directors

In terms of section 282 of the Companies Act 1985, every private company requires to have at least one director. Public companies, unless registered prior to November 1, 1929, require to have at least two directors. Although it follows from the foregoing provision that private companies require a single director only, Article 64 of Table A provides that the minimum number of directors shall be two. Accordingly, if Table A is adopted without amendment of this provision, a private company, in order to comply with its Articles, will require two directors. Where it is intended that a sole director be appointed then Article 64 of Table A will require to be adjusted accordingly or, in terms of the Article, an ordinary resolution of the members of the company will be required approving the appointment of a single director. 6.1.1

On his appointment to the board of an incorporated company, a director will require to sign a statutory form of consent (Companies Form 288a). This form is also used to intimate the director's appointment and certain prescribed particulars to the Registrar of Companies. As we have seen the director's name and the same prescribed particulars also require to be entered in the company's own register of directors maintained in terms of section 288 of the Companies Act 1985. The completion of Companies Form 288a will be considered in greater detail later in this chapter.

It is essential to appreciate that a person may be held to be a director of a company for the purposes of the Companies Acts even although he is not referred to as such and despite the fact that none of the required formalities may have been complied with. In terms of section 741 of the 1985 Act, a director includes any person occupying the position of director by whatever name he is called. Accordingly, the register of directors maintained by a company or by the Registrar of Companies cannot, of themselves, be taken as conclusive evidence of those persons who may be held to be directors in law. Further confusion results from the varied terminology adopted in practice with regard to company directors and indeed in relation to the use of the word "director" generally.

As stated, the use of the word "director" is not compulsory. For example, many directors are referred to as members of a management committee or as council members or even as governors. This is particularly common with companies limited by guarantee or with charitable objects where the term "director" may be thought to be too commercial in tone. Equally, certain paid employees or officials may not be directors in law even although referred to as, for example, managing directors, or, as is often the case with local authorities, directors of administration or the like. An individual's designation therefore cannot always be taken, by itself, as establishing whether or not he bears the legal duties and responsibilities of a company director.

6.1.2 The Companies Acts do not dictate any specific qualifications which are required by company directors. As we shall see however some individuals may be disqualified from acting as directors in certain circumstances. Generally, however, any person including companies and Scottish firms can be appointed as a director. In the past it was common to provide in the Articles of Association of a company that its directors had to hold a minimum number of the company's shares. Where such a provision applies then, in terms of section 291 of the 1985 Act, the director must acquire his qualification shares within two months of his appointment or such shorter period as the Articles may specify. If the director fails to comply then his position is automatically vacated. Share qualifications are still encountered on occasion but, as indicated, these have become unfashionable.

One further restriction on directors may be mentioned here. Section 293 of the 1985 Act sets an age limit for directors of public companies or their subsidiaries of 70 years. This age limit gives rise to the requirement that a director states his date of birth when completing Companies Forms 10 or 288a. The age limit can be dispensed with by ordinary resolution of the company provided that special notice of the resolution is given to the members of the company.

Categories of Directors

6.2 Those persons who are held to be directors in law may be divided into a number of categories. A particularly common distinction is between executive and non-executive directors. Executive directors ordinarily means those holding executive office within the company and who, as a result, are generally also employees of the company. A non-executive director on the other hand will ordinarily perform his duty to the company through attendance at board meetings or meetings of committees of the board. It is important to note that the statutory code does not draw any distinction between the legal and other responsibilities of executive and non-executive directors.

Reference is also sometimes made to alternate, shadow and associate directors. An alternate director is an individual nominated by a director of a company to attend and vote at board meetings in the absence of that director. Detailed provision is made for the appointment, removal and powers of alternate directors under Articles 65–69 of Table A. Again, in law, an alternate director will have the same duties and responsibilities as the director who appointed him.

The term shadow director is specifically defined by section 741 of the Companies Act 1985 as "a person in accordance with whose directions or instructions the directors of the company are accustomed to act". It is specifically provided that a person shall not be deemed to be a shadow director by reason only that the directors act on advice given by him in a professional capacity. Here we have a clear example of individuals who may not have subscribed the required Companies Form, who may not be registered in either the company's own register of directors or in the public register, but who nevertheless will be deemed to be directors in law. This definition coupled with the introduction of the concept of wrongful trading has caused some concern to those dealing with companies generally and, in particular, to those investing in companies. This will be considered in more detail later in this chapter.

Finally, reference is sometimes made to associate directors, that is individuals who hold senior positions within a company or who advise the company on particular matters but who do not ordinarily sit on the board of the company. Whether or not these individuals fall within the legal definition of company directors will be largely dependent upon circumstances.

Appointment, Resignation and Removal of Directors

As we have seen, the first directors on incorporation of a company 6.3.1
require to be specified on Companies Form 10 when this is submitted to the Registrar of Companies. Each director requires to sign the form consenting to act as a director of the company and giving prescribed particulars regarding him or herself. These include the director's full name, any former name, residential address, occupation, nationality, date of birth and any other directorships held by the director either at the time of appointment or in the preceding five years. As indicated, following incorporation, any change in the particulars of the directors of the company requires to be intimated to the Registrar of Companies on Companies Form 288a. The same form is used to deal with the appointment of additional directors (who require to sign the form consenting to act as directors). Companies Form 228b is used for the purpose of intimating the resignation of any director. All appointments, changes or resignations require to be notified within 14 days from the date of the relevant change.

The Companies Acts contain little or no provision regarding the appointment of company directors other than to specify that, in the case of public companies, the appointment of two or more directors should be dealt with by separate resolutions unless the appointments are agreed upon unanimously. Various Articles of Table A do however contain more detailed provisions regarding appointment of directors and these are frequently adopted with little or no amendment. In terms of Table A, the members of a company may, by ordinary resolution, appoint any person who is willing to act to be a director of the company. The existing directors may also appoint a director either to fill a vacancy or as an additional director provided that such appointment does not cause the number of directors to exceed any maximum number fixed by the Articles. A director appointed by the board of directors holds office only until the next following Annual General Meeting of the company at which he requires to be re-appointed.

6.3.2 Articles 73 and following of Table A contain provision for the retirement of directors by rotation. In terms of Article 73, at the first Annual General Meeting of the company all directors retire from office. At each subsequent Annual General Meeting one-third of the directors who are subject to retirement by rotation, or if their number is not three or a multiple of three, the number nearest to one-third shall retire from office. The members of the company then have the opportunity of deciding whether or not to reappoint those directors retiring by rotation. In terms of Article 84, a managing or executive director is not to be subject to retirement by rotation. It is important to note that if the retiring director is willing to act he shall be deemed to have been reappointed unless either it is resolved not to fill his vacancy or a resolution for the appointment of the director is put to the meeting and lost. As a general rule, those directors who are to retire at any particular Annual General Meeting shall be those who have been longest in office. Where directors were appointed on the same date, those to retire shall (unless they otherwise agree among themselves) be determined by lot. If the directors fail to reach agreement, the members of the company may determine the basis for retirement by ordinary resolution.

Under Table A, no person other than a director retiring by rotation can be appointed a director unless either he is recommended by the directors of the company or, not less than 14 nor more than 35 clear days before the date appointed for the meeting, notice executed by a member qualified to vote at the meeting has been given to the company of the intention to propose that person for appointment. The notice must state the particulars requiring to be given regarding that director, together with confirmation of the director's willingness to be appointed.

As indicated previously, it is common in the case of private limited companies to amend the provisions regarding the retirement of directors by rotation. These provisions are generally viewed as being inappropriate in a small company where the members and directors are frequently the same individuals.

Article 81 of Table A contains provisions regarding thc disqualification and removal of directors. In particular, the office of a director is to be vacated in the event of the director being prohibited by law from being a director, becoming bankrupt or making any arrangement or composition with his creditors, suffering from mental disorder or resigning his office by notice to the company. A director may also be removed if he shall, for more than six months, have been absent from meetings of the directors without the permission of the other directors. It is important to note that the removal of a director as such does not necessarily mean that he automatically ceases to be an employee of the company. 6.3.3

In this regard it is important both for the company and the individual concerned to make absolutely clear whether or not a removal or resignation relates to appointment as a director and to any office held as an employee of the company. Where a director also holds office as an employee of the company, he is entitled to the usual rights of employees conferred in terms of the Employment Rights Act 1996. He may, for example, be entitled to claim compensation for unfair dismissal or redundancy against the company.

In terms of section 303 of the 1985 Act, a company may, by ordinary resolution, remove a director before the expiration of his period of office if such a period has been fixed. Such a resolution may be passed and will be effective notwithstanding anything in the Articles of Association of the company or in any agreement between the company and the director concerned. The apparently clear terms of this section can be effectively avoided by giving to a particular director sufficient voting rights to enable him to secure his position on the board and block any resolution for his removal. It is clear from reported cases that the courts will not accept any provision of the Articles which states, for example, that Mr Henderson is not to be removed as a director of the company. If on the other hand, the Articles provide that, on a resolution to remove him, Mr Henderson is to have, for example, 10 votes for each share held by him, then he may effectively block such a resolution notwithstanding that he may only hold a minority shareholding in the company. Nowadays, it is perhaps more common to protect from removal directors who are also minority shareholders by dividing the share capital of the company into various classes and attaching to each class specific rights, including the right to appoint a director. Suitable provisions may also be made to protect the individual director in a written agreement between the shareholders of the company.

In terms of section 303 where it is sought to remove a director by ordinary resolution of the company, it is necessary to give special notice of that resolution. This has been considered in Chapter 5. In addition, following upon section 304, the director who is to be removed has a right to protest against his removal and to be heard at the meeting called to consider the resolution for his removal. The director may make representations to the company against his removal and may insist upon these being circulated to members. Where it is intended to remove a director in contentious circumstances and reliance is placed upon section 303, then the statutory provisions (along with the company's articles) should be carefully consulted before any step is taken. In order that matters may be dealt with fairly, it is suggested that copies of the sections should be sent to the director in question along with a copy of the proposed notice calling the required meeting.

Disqualification of Directors

6.4 In terms of the Company Directors Disqualification Act 1986, a person may be disqualified from acting as a director of a company or from being concerned or otherwise taking part whether directly or indirectly in the promotion, formation or management of a company unless expressly authorised on application to the court. Breach of a disqualification order is a criminal offence and may lead to the imposition of a fine or imprisonment. The person concerned may also incur personal liability for company debts incurred during the period of breach.

Disqualification may arise in a number of circumstances which are set out in the Act and which may be summarised as follows.

(a) Where a person is convicted for an indictable offence in connection with the promotion, formation, management or liquidation of a company.

(b) Where a person is in persistent default of his duties under the Companies Acts to file documents with the Registrar of Companies.

(c) In cases of wrongful or fraudulent trading under section 213 or 214 of the Insolvency Act 1986 or generally in cases involving fraud on the winding-up of a company.

(d) Where a person is shown to be unfit to be involved in the management of a company. Section 9 and Schedule 1 to the Act set out matters relevant in determining whether or not a person is unfit for the purpose including, in particular, the following:

(i) any misfeasance or breach of any fiduciary or other duty by the director in relation to the company;

(ii) any misapplication or retention of company funds or property;
(iii) failure to comply with the requirements to maintain proper accounting records and registers and to prepare and to submit annual returns;
(iv) in cases of insolvency the extent of the director's responsibility for such insolvency;
(v) failing to prepare the statement of affairs required following upon receivership or liquidation.

Application for a disqualification order under the Act can be made only by the Secretary of State or, with his authority, the Official Receiver in England and Wales. A court may however make a disqualification order when considering cases of wrongful or fraudulent trading. An order may be made for a period of between two and 15 years. Generally the making of disqualification orders has arisen from adverse reports made by company receivers or liquidators to the Department of Trade and Industry following upon a company's insolvency. In terms of the Act, every administrator, administrative receiver and liquidator in respect of an insolvent company must submit to the Secretary of State a report indicating whether, in his opinion, any person involved as a director or shadow director of the company has conducted himself in a manner rendering him unfit to be concerned in the management of a company.

Finally it should be noted that, in terms of section 11 of the Act, no undischarged bankrupt can hold the position of company director or be involved, directly or indirectly, in the promotion, formation or management of a company except with the leave of the court.

Directors' Service Contracts and Remuneration

In terms of Article 82 of Table A, directors are entitled to such 6.5
remuneration as the company may, by ordinary resolution, determine. This is not generally taken as applying to any entitlement to remuneration arising from an employment contract held by a director. Any payment made by way of directors' fees on the other hand does require to be approved by the company itself in general meeting. It is essential that any such payments are so approved as, failing approval, they may be open to challenge at a later date by members of the company or by a liquidator.

It is common for directors who hold executive office to enter into a written contract with the company making provision for the terms of their employment. Such contracts are generally referred to as directors' service contracts. They are, however, in essence merely contracts of employment between the director and the company concerned. In terms of section 319 of the 1985 Act, no service contract or contract of employment for a director is to exceed a term of five years unless approved by the members of the company in general meeting. In terms of section 318 of the Act, any service contract for a director or, where such a contract is unwritten, a memorandum setting out the principal terms of the agreement, must be kept by the company at its registered office, the place where its register of members is kept or its principal place of business provided that this is within that part of the country in which the company is registered. Any member of the company is entitled to inspect such contracts.

The arrangements made with regard to directors' service contracts frequently give rise to difficulties. Although the company may be entitled, by ordinary resolution, to remove a director of the company, the statutory section providing for this (section 303) makes it clear that the right to remove is without prejudice to any claim for damages or compensation which might be available to the director in question. Where a director has been granted a service contract for an extended period of perhaps five years he may be entitled to substantial compensation for breach of contract on the part of the company. As a result, when considering the interests of the company, it is prudent to restrict the terms of any such contract to the minimum practical period. There will of course require to be balanced against this the need to give some security to executive directors in the interests of securing their services.

Over and above the usual provisions of an employment contract, a director's service contract may also make provision for a restrictive covenant in terms of which the director undertakes not to compete with the business of the company following termination of the contract for a specified period. Such clauses are, of course, not exclusive to company directors but are perhaps more regularly found in directors' service contracts. The law has been wary regarding the enforcement of such contractual provisions, there being a general view that it is not in the public interest to allow such terms to be enforced for extended periods. The contractual provisions will be strictly interpreted against the company seeking to apply them and if any part of the provisions is deemed to be unreasonable then the whole covenant may be unenforceable. This has led to a number of attempts to draft clauses which are stated to be subject to adjustment in the event of any part of the clause being held to be unreasonable. There must however be some doubt whether or not these clauses are themselves enforceable. The best solution from the point of view of any company wishing to include such a provision is to accept a reasonable and realistic restriction only and not to seek too extensive a restraint on the director concerned in case this should render the clause unenforceable. Generally, periods of up to one year will be acceptable (although this cannot be universally guaranteed) with the covenant applying to the geographical area within which the company regularly operates. Any attempt to go beyond these bounds *may* be struck down as being unreasonable. Another mechanism is to provide for an extended notice period on the part of the director.

A simple form of service contract is contained in Schedule 12.

Directors' Powers, Duties and Responsibilities

As we have seen, article 70 of Table A delegates the power to manage the company's affairs to the directors of the company from time to time. This delegation is generally subject only to the terms of the Companies Acts, the Memorandum and Articles of Association of the company and any directions given by special resolution of the members of the company itself. Directors are given express power in terms of Article 71 to appoint any person to be the agent of the company for such purposes and on such conditions as they may determine. They are further authorised in terms of Article 72 to delegate their powers to any committee consisting of one or more directors or to a managing director or any other director holding executive office again on such terms as they consider desirable. Following upon the delegation of powers contained in Article 70, the management of the company on a day-to-day basis is generally removed from the ambit of the members of the company itself who are not then, in the ordinary case, able to intervene in such day-to-day management. As indicated previously, this delegation of powers lies at the very heart of company law and it is essential that all those involved with companies appreciate and accept the implications of these provisions. 6.6.1

As is commonly the case in our law, the granting of powers is generally coupled with the acceptance of legal duties and responsibilities by the party concerned. The overriding duty of the director is to act in good faith in what he considers to be the best interests of the company. He must show the highest loyalty and good faith to the company. He must act in the company's interests and without regard to any collateral purpose or personal motives. He must display such skill as his personal qualifications warrant and accordingly more will be expected of an experienced man of business than in the case of an amateur. Apart from these rather intangible continuing duties of loyalty and good faith, a director's duties are often of an intermittent nature, including, in particular, regular attendance at board meetings. The degree of diligence expected will depend upon the facts of each individual case; the same general principles applying to both executive and non-executive directors. 6.6.2

The obligation on directors to act for the benefit of the company is generally taken to mean the long term interest of the company as a whole. This includes the interests of both present *and* future shareholders of the company. Section 309 of the Companies Act 1985 also requires directors to have regard to the interests of the company's employees although this duty is owed not to the employees themselves but to the company who alone can enforce this duty.

6.6.3 The rules by which a company is to be governed are now commonly referred to as the principles of corporate governance. Following the collapse of a number of listed companies, a committee under the chairmanship of Sir Adrian Cadbury was set up in May 1991 by, amongst others, the London Stock Exchange and the accounting profession to address concerns relating to the management of listed companies. The Cadbury Report published in May 1992 confirmed that shareholders' controls over company boards and auditors were inefficient, boards were seen to be dominated by the executive directors, whereas the non-executive directors (although approved by shareholders) were nominated by the chief executive whom they were intended to monitor. Auditors were also found to have a closer relation with the board than with the shareholders.

To address these concerns the Cadbury Report proposed a code of best practice to be complied with by all boards of listed companies. The principles established by Cadbury have a wider application however and should be carefully considered by directors of any company, including private companies, when the board is distinct from the shareholders.

Following the Cadbury Report, a further committee known as the Greenbury Committee was set up in order to review the area of directors' remuneration. The Greenbury Committee published its recommendations in July 1995. Again, although these relate specifically to listed companies, they may be relevant to larger private companies in setting the standard of good practice which boards should follow.

A detailed consideration of Cadbury and Greenbury is beyond the scope of this work but brief reference may usefully be made to one or two of the principles they established.

Code of Practice

6.6.4 The principles on which the code is based are those of openness on the part of companies, integrity in their dealings and financial reporting and accountability of directors to shareholders through the quality of information provided. The board should meet regularly, retain full and effective control over the company and monitor the executive management. There should be a clearly accepted division between the responsibilities of the chairman and chief executive, which will ensure a balance of power and authority, such that no one individual has unfettered powers of decision-making. The non-executive directors should be of such calibre and number that their views carry sufficient weight in the board's decisions. All directors should have access to the advice and services of the company secretary, who is responsible to the board for ensuring that the board procedures are followed and that applicable rules and regulations are complied with. Directors' service contracts should not exceed three years without shareholders' approval. Executive directors' pay should be subject to the recommendations of a remuneration committee made up wholly or mainly of non-executive directors. It is the board's duty to present a balanced and understandable assessment of the company's position. The board should ensure that an objective and professional relationship is maintained with the auditors. The board should establish an audit committee of non-executive directors with written terms of reference which deal clearly with its authority and duties.

Greenbury

The Greenbury Committee recommended that a remuneration 6.6.5
committee should be established to determine the company's policy on executive directors' remuneration and specific remuneration packages for each of the executive directors, including pension rights and any compensation payments. Remuneration committees should consist exclusively of non-executive directors with no personal financial interests or potential conflict, other than as shareholders, in the matter to be decided.

Fraudulent trading

Section 213 of the Insolvency Act 1986 provides that if in the course 6.7.1
of a winding-up it appears that any business of the company has been carried out with intent to defraud creditors of the company or creditors of any person or for any fraudulent purpose, the court, on the application of the liquidator, may declare that any *person* (*i.e.* not just a director) who was knowingly a party to the carrying-on of the business in such a manner is to be personally liable to make such contribution to the company's assets as the court thinks proper.

Fraudulent trading is notoriously difficult to prove; many directors accused of fraudulent trading successfully managing to claim that they have not carried on the business with the intent to defraud but rather that they have believed that by continuing to trade they could "pull the business round" and put the company back into profit. The courts in recent years have been less inclined to accept such arguments and have shown a willingness to include within the definition of "fraudulent" that which at one time they did not feel came within the narrow definition of that term. However the introduction of the concept of wrongful trading has led to a reduction in fraudulent trading claims. There may, however, be occasions when it is still necessary to rely on the fraudulent trading provisions, for example where someone other than a director (or shadow director) is involved in the conduct complained of.

Section 212 of the Insolvency Act 1986 contains a parallel provision with regard to misappropriation of funds or breach of trust by those connected with a company. It applies to any officer of the company (for example the company secretary), a liquidator, administrator, receiver or any person who has taken part in or been concerned with the promotion, formation or management of the company. If it appears that any such individual has misapplied or retained or become accountable for any money or other property of the company or been guilty of any misfeasance or breach of any fiduciary or other duty in relation to the company, then the court, on the application of the liquidator or any creditor or contributory, may compel the individual concerned:

(a) to repay, restore or account for the money or property or any part of it with interest at such rate as the court thinks fit; or
(b) to contribute such sum to the assets of the company by way of compensation as the court thinks fit.

Where application is made by a contributory, the leave of the court is required.

Wrongful trading

6.7.2 In terms of section 214 of the Insolvency Act 1986, the court may, on the application of a company's liquidator, require one or more of the past or present directors of the company to make such contribution from their own personal assets to the company's assets as the court deems proper. The section applies where (1) the company has gone into insolvent liquidation; (2) at some time before the commencement of the winding up of the company (but after April 28, 1986) that person knew or ought to have concluded that there was no reasonable prospect that the company would avoid going into insolvent liquidation; and (3) that person was a director of the company at the time.

The statutory provision applies with equal force to a shadow director. In terms of section 714 of the Companies Act 1985, a shadow director is defined as a person in accordance with whose directions or instructions the directors of a company are accustomed to act. A person is not, however, deemed to be a shadow director by reason only that the directors act on advice given by him in a professional capacity. The exact scope of this saving has yet to be finally established, but clearly some care will require to be exercised by those engaged to advise the directors of a company which is, or may be, insolvent. The professional advice of accountants, lawyers, bankers and the like would clearly appear to fall within the statutory proviso. Where, however, the professional advisor also takes an active part in the company's management, he runs the risk of falling foul of the provision of section 214. Particular caution will require to be exercised by lending institutions who nominate a representative to a company board precisely in order that he may advise them should the company run into difficulties and so that he may take appropriate steps, as and when required, in order to protect the lender's investment. Anyone acting in such a capacity should ensure that he is adequately protected either by way of indemnity from the body appointing him or by means of suitable indemnity insurance.

The court will refuse to comply with the liquidator's request for payment of compensation to the company by a director if it is satisfied that the director, after knowing of the inevitability of insolvent liquidation, took every step with a view to minimising the potential losses of the creditors of the company which he ought to have taken. Subsection (4) provides that the facts which a director ought to know or ascertain, the conclusions which he ought to reach and the steps which he ought to take are those which would be known or ascertained, or reached or taken by a reasonably diligent person having both (a) the general knowledge, skill and experience that may reasonably be expected of a person carrying out the same functions as are carried out by that director in relation to the company; and (b) the general knowledge, skill and experience which that director has.

This test is both objective and subjective in its content. A skilled director, a man of particular talents, will be judged by his own high standards in terms of subheading (b) and in this respect the criteria applies subjectively. An individual of less than average ability will not, however, be able to plead this in his defence as he is required, in terms of subheading (a), to comply with the objective standard of the reasonable director.

The new provisions with regard to wrongful trading apply only in 6.7.3
the event of a company going into insolvent liquidation. A director's first concern therefore should be to ascertain whether or not his company is and continues to be solvent. Where a company is wound up, and its assets are insufficient to pay its whole debts and the expenses of its winding-up, then the winding-up is deemed to be an insolvent liquidation. It may in some cases be difficult for directors to ascertain whether or not their company is technically insolvent and whether or not such a liquidation is in prospect. For example, a company's assets may realise substantially less on liquidation than they appear to be worth in terms of the company's annual accounts when that company is a going concern. In particular, the value of goodwill and work in progress may fall dramatically on a company's winding-up. Many commercial contracts contain a clause terminating the

contract in the event of a company's liquidation and this also can affect the value of the company's assets.

In order to ascertain whether or not his company is solvent a director should satisfy himself firstly that the company is paying its liabilities as they fall due or shortly thereafter and that it can continue to do so in the foreseeable future; secondly that the aggregate liabilities of the company, including contingent and prospective liabilities do not exceed the total value of the company's assets; and thirdly, that if the company were to go into liquidation, the assets would be sufficient to settle all liabilities and the costs of the liquidation. As indicated, this last test will generally be the hardest to satisfy.

Having ascertained whether or not the company is solvent, and assuming that a satisfactory answer has been obtained, it will be necessary for directors to continuously monitor their company's performance in order to ensure that they have adequate warning of any difficulties which may occur. This will normally entail attendance at regular board meetings of the company and ensuring the availability of regular and up-to-date management and audited accounts. In any case where it appears to directors that their company may be insolvent and an insolvent liquidation may be in prospect then, as a bare minimum, the directors should forthwith convene a board meeting of the company to consider in detail its financial position. Advice should be sought from the company's solicitors and auditors as a matter of urgency in order to ascertain what steps, if any, ought to be taken to remedy the position. If the situation cannot be quickly rectified then it may be necessary to consider arranging for the appointment of a receiver, an administrator or even for the company's immediate winding-up.

6.7.4 There can now be little doubt that the statutory provisions with regard to wrongful trading have had a material impact upon the management of limited companies. Sadly, as is often the case, statutory provisions which are intended to catch the rogue director in fact cause some difficulties for even the most responsible directors where their companies do not have a substantial underlying capital worth. For example, the statutory rules may make it difficult for a charitable company relying upon a discretionary annual grant to undertake longer term liabilities such as a lease of property or long-term employment contracts. Nevertheless, it is suggested that the statutory provisions have given some impetus to improving management methods in a large number of companies and have encouraged companies to take an earlier decision regarding winding-up rather than continuing to trade incurring further liabilities.

As has been indicated previously, it is now possible to obtain directors' and officers' liability insurance cover which, in some cases, purports to include cover against a claim of wrongful trading. One would expect to pay several thousand pounds per annum for the minimum of cover although the level of premium will clearly depend upon the exact circumstances of each case. Normally a company's professional advisers will be able to obtain quotations for directors if provided with a copy of the company's accounts for the last few financial years, a copy of the company's Memorandum and Articles of Association and details regarding the present board of directors. The Institute of Directors can also offer guidance in this regard. Considerable caution requires to be exercised in determining whether or not such insurance cover should be taken out. The details of the cover provided and the various items excepted from the cover should be carefully considered. In the case of wrongful trading in particular, there is, of course, the possibility that as a company slips into financial difficulties the annual premiums rise to an unaffordable level just at the time when cover is most required. As noted previously, where such cover is taken out this fact requires to be disclosed in the annual accounts of the company.

Transactions Involving Directors

Part X of the Companies Act 1985 contains a number of provisions intended to enforce fair dealing by directors. These provisions include, in particular, a prohibition on tax-free payments being made to directors, the requirement for payments or transfer of property by way of compensation for loss of office to be disclosed to and approved by the members of the company in general meeting, the requirement for disclosure of any payment to be made to the director at the time of a takeover as consideration for or in connection with his retirement from office and the provisions regarding directors' service contracts noted previously. The following further provisions should also be noted. 6.8.1

Subject to a number of exceptions, a company is prohibited by section 320 of the 1985 Act from entering into any arrangement whereby a director of the company or of its holding company or a person connected with such a director acquires or is to acquire one or more non-cash assets above a prescribed value from the company or whereby the company acquires such an asset from the director or a person so connected with him unless that arrangement is first approved by an ordinary resolution of the company in general meeting. For the purposes of the section the prescribed value of a non-cash asset falling within the section is a sum exceeding £100,000 or, if less, 10 per cent of the company's asset value subject to a minimum of £2,000. 6.8.2

In terms of section 323 of the 1985 Act, directors are prohibited from dealing in share options in respect of their company where those 6.8.3

shares are listed on a Stock Exchange, whether in Great Britain or elsewhere.

6.8.4 Section 330 of the 1985 Act prohibits a company, subject to various exceptions, from making a loan to a director of the company or its holding company or entering into any guarantee or providing any security in connection with the loan made to such a director. The Act also prohibits the making of quasi-loans to directors; a quasi-loan being defined as a transaction under which one party ("the creditor") agrees to pay a sum for another ("the borrower") or agrees to reimburse expenditure incurred by one party for another in terms that the borrower will reimburse the creditor. The prohibition in relation to quasi-loans applies only to public companies or a member of a group of companies which includes a public company. The Act provides various exceptions to the foregoing provisions authorising, in particular, short term quasi-loans of up to £5,000, loans not exceeding £5,000, minor business transactions again not exceeding £5,000 and funding provided to enable a director to meet expenditure in carrying out his duties to the company.

6.8.5 In terms of section 109 of the Companies Act 1989, substituting a new section 322A in the 1985 Act, where a transaction is entered into between a company and either one of its directors or a person connected with such a director, then if the directors have exceeded their powers in entering the transaction the transaction will be voidable at the instance of the company. Furthermore the parties to the transaction, and any director who authorised it, will be liable to the company not only to make good any loss which the company may have suffered, but also to account to the company for any gain which they have made as a result, directly or indirectly, of the transaction.

The foregoing is a summary only of the statutory provisions and these should be carefully consulted and, where appropriate, legal advice sought in any case where a transaction between a company and its directors is envisaged.

The Company Secretary

6.9.1 Section 283 of the Companies Act 1985 provides that every company has to have a secretary. There is no reason why a director of a company cannot be its secretary but the Act prohibits a sole director from also acting as secretary. Likewise no company is to have as its secretary a corporation the sole director of which is the sole director of the company or vice versa. Where, in terms of the Act, anything is required or authorised to be done by or to the secretary it may, if for any reason the secretary is incapable of acting, be done by or to any assistant or depute secretary or by any officer of the company authorised generally or specially by the directors for that purpose.

As we have seen the first secretary of the company requires to be intimated prior to incorporation on Companies Form 10. Any change in the office holder also requires to be intimated within 14 days of such change using Companies Forms 288a and b. In terms of Article 99 of Table A, which is generally adopted without qualification, the directors of the company are given authority to appoint the secretary at such remuneration and upon such conditions as they may think fit. Any secretary may likewise be removed by the directors.

In the case of a public company the directors of the company are under an obligation, in terms of section 286 of the 1985 Act, to take all reasonable steps to secure that the secretary of the company is a person who appears to them to have the requisite knowledge and experience to discharge the functions of secretary of the company. The Act lays down a number of specific qualifications which must be met by the secretary of a public company. Generally any solicitor and members of the principal accountancy bodies are qualified to act. There is no such requirement for particular qualifications in the case of a private company.

Duties and responsibilities of company secretary

As an officer of the company, the secretary has the responsibility 6.9.2
of ensuring that the company complies with the requirements of the Companies Acts. In view of the ever-increasing complexity of the statutory code, this is becoming an evermore burdensome task. Where there is a breach of the statutory provisions, the secretary, again being an officer of the company, may be liable along with the directors for any penalty payable in terms of the Act. Generally, however, the principal responsibility for the management of the company's affairs rests with its directors with the secretary acting in an administrative capacity only. Because of the complexity of the law it is not now recommended that an unqualified individual lightly take on the task of company secretary. Instead it is generally advisable for the company's solicitors or accountants to take on this role. Clearly this will involve the incurring of professional fees to the firm concerned. Frequently, however, firms will carry out this work for a nominal charge only, especially where this is incidental to other advice and assistance being given.

Although the responsibilities of secretaries, as with those of directors, vary tremendously in practice, the secretary will be closely involved with all company meetings, whether these are board meetings or meetings of the members of the company. As might be expected, the secretary is usually responsible for the maintenance of the company's minute books, statutory registers and other records. The secretary will be expected to deal with the calling of all meetings and the lodging of all intimations and forms required by the Registrar of

Companies. Where accountants or solicitors are engaged to act as company secretary, these services can be provided on a number of levels with the costs varying accordingly. At one end of the spectrum solicitors may take the legal title of secretary but may simply deal with the annual formalities of preparing the paperwork required for the annual general meeting and lodging the required accounts and annual return. The fee for this work will generally be nominal. Alternatively, agents can provide a full secretarial service including attendance at all company meetings, issuing agendas and notices, preparation of minutes and carrying through all the administrative work of a company secretary. In these cases the costs may be substantial, being entirely dependent on the level of involvement required.

CHAPTER 7

SHARES AND SHAREHOLDERS

The Members

The members of a limited company are the owners of the company with the division of that ownership generally being directly referrable to the number of shares held in the company. The holding of shares (or the membership of a guarantee company) gives the member no direct right to claim any part of the assets of the company itself. The right of the member is an incorporeal right to a share of the company itself as a legal entity. Generally, membership of a company carries with it a number of specific rights, including in particular the right to share in any profits which the company agrees to distribute amongst its members, a right to vote at meetings of the members of the company and a right to share in the capital of the company on its being wound up. We will consider these rights in detail later in this chapter. 7.1.1

Membership of a company may be constituted in two ways. Firstly, one can become a member of a company by subscribing the Memorandum of Association of the company in terms of which, as we have seen, the subscribers agree to become members of the company immediately upon its incorporation. In this case, membership is constituted automatically on the incorporation of the company with no further legal requirement being called for. If one is not a subscriber to the Memorandum, then in order to become a member of the company a person must agree to become a member and must be entered as such in the company's Register of Members. In this case, therefore, there must not only be an agreement to become a member, but also registration of membership by the company. It should be noted that although registration is not an essential requirement of a subscriber to the Memorandum of Association becoming a member of the company, such an individual should be registered as a member immediately following incorporation of the company. As a result, the Register of Members of a company should be a definitive statement of those individuals who are currently members of the company in law. 7.1.2

Clearly, there are many cases where, for example, an existing member of a company may agree to transfer his shares to a third party but where that third party has not, at that time, been registered as a member. In this case the transferor will remain a member of the company until the transfer is registered although between the transferor and the transferee, the transferor may hold such membership in trust for the transferee. Where the document of transfer requires to be stamped prior to registration, there may be considerable delay in the updating of the register. Where it is anticipated that this period may last for some time, as, for example, where the stamp duty payable requires to be adjudicated by the Inland Revenue, the transferee may seek to obtain further written assurances from the transferor that the transferor will vote at meetings and otherwise act in accordance with the transferee's instructions pending such registration.

Where a company fails to register a transfer or allotment of shares or improperly delays in removing an individual's name from the Register of Members, it is open to the aggrieved party to petition the court for an order correcting the register. The court can, in addition to ordering rectification of the register, make an order compensating any party who has suffered loss as a result of the company's failure.

7.1.3 In the case of a company limited by shares, the member will be bound to pay over either to the company in the case of an allotment of shares by the company or to the member transferring the shares, the subscription or sale price or such part thereof as has been agreed between the parties. This may be distinguished from the position in relation to a guarantee company where, in the ordinary case, the member agrees only to contribute such sum not exceeding an agreed figure as may be necessary to clear the debts of the company on its being wound up. As we have seen, the maximum liability is generally a nominal one of perhaps £1.00 to £5.00, although there is no reason in law why this figure should not be as high as the parties might agree. In the case of either a guarantee company or a company limited by shares the sole obligation of the member is to pay the amount, if any, unpaid on his shares, or, in the case of a guarantee company, the unpaid amount of the member's agreed contribution.

Allotment of Shares

7.2.1 As indicated, shares in a company can be acquired either by allotment from the company itself or by the transfer of existing shares from a member of the company. In order to enable a company to allot shares, it must first have registered the required share capital. Thus a company may be incorporated with an authorised share capital of £100 divided into 100 ordinary shares of £1.00 each. At least one of these shares will have been taken up by the subscriber to the Memorandum. On incorporation therefore, a single member company might have an authorised share capital of £100 and an issued share capital of £1.00. The company will have a further 99 unissued ordinary shares which can be allotted as appropriate. If the company wishes to allot more than 100 shares in total then it will require to increase its authorised share capital. The mechanism for increasing share capital is dealt with in Chapter 8.

Assuming that a company has unissued shares available for 7.2.2
allotment then such allotment may be effected either by resolution of the members of the company or by resolution of the directors of the company. In either case, careful consideration will require to be given to any rights of pre-emption which may be available to existing members either in terms of the Articles of Association of the company or in terms of the Companies Act 1985. In the case of an allotment by the directors of the company, it is also necessary to consider whether or not the directors have obtained the necessary authority from the members of the company enabling them to allot such shares.

As we have seen in Chapter 3, sections 89–95 of the Companies Act 1985 provide that the existing members of a company are entitled to take up any further shares which the company seeks to issue in proportion to their existing shareholdings. The purpose of this statutory provision is to protect shareholders against the watering down of their interest in a company by the allotment of shares to third parties or to other members of the company. As we have seen, it is possible for the members of a company to agree to waive their statutory rights either in their entirety or by the substitution of alternative rights within the Articles of Association of the company. Such waiver of statutory rights requires a special resolution of the members of the company. It is essential, therefore, that, prior to allotting any shares, care is taken to check whether or not the necessary pre-emption rights have been waived, failing which the shares will require to be offered first to the existing members in accordance with the terms of either the Act or the Articles of Association.

Assuming that the issue of pre-emption rights has been satisfactorily 7.2.3
resolved, it is then necessary to determine whether or not the directors themselves may allot shares or whether the members of the company require to authorise this. In terms of section 80 of the Companies Act 1985, the directors of a company cannot allot shares unless authorised to do so either by the Articles of Association of the company or by ordinary resolution of the members of the company. The authority will ordinarily expire after a period of five years following the date of adoption of the Articles or the date of the relevant resolution or such shorter period as may be specified in the authority unless the members have passed an elective resolution to the effect that such authority should persist.

The form of resolution ordinarily adopted to enable directors to deal with the allotment of shares without reference to pre-emption rights is contained in paragraph 3.3.3.

Agreement to Become a Member

7.3 As indicated above, the first requirement of becoming a member of a company is that there be agreement to such membership. In the case of an allotment of shares by the company, this agreement will ordinarily be evidenced by a letter of application addressed by the member to the company requesting the allotment of a specific number of shares at a specific price. This "offer" is then accepted and made binding by the company issuing a formal letter of allotment.

Membership will not however be attained until such allotment has been registered. Membership of a guarantee company is generally evidenced by a form of consent whereby the member agrees to take up membership and to contribute up to the agreed sum if this is subsequently required. A form of consent to become a member is included within Schedule 13.

Allotment of Shares to the Public

7.4 Section 57 of the Financial Services Act 1986 prohibits any person, including a private company, from issuing or causing to be issued any advertisement offering shares of the company unless such advertisement has been approved by a person authorised under the Act. The Secretary of State can nevertheless approve such advertisements in very limited circumstances particularly where they appear to "have a private character" or where issued to persons sufficiently expert to understand the risks involved. The word "advertisement" is defined broadly to include not only advertisement in the general sense, but also any catalogue or circular or "other document". Offers of shares in a private company to the public including any section of the public, members of a company or clients of the person making the offer are also governed by the Public Offers of Securities Regulations 1995. These require the preparation, publication and registration of a prospectus for the shares setting out detailed information regarding the shares and the company itself. Such offers or advertisements are generally outwith the scope of this work, but where these are proposed, it is essential that legal advice be obtained prior to any steps being taken with regard to the proposed offer or advertisement, as a breach of the relevant rules may give rise to both civil and criminal proceedings.

Transfer of Shares

7.5.1 As indicated, the second method of acquiring shares in a company is by the transfer of previously allotted shares from a member of the company. Such a transfer must be effected by a proper Instrument of

Transfer. The usual form adopted is a Stock Transfer Form in terms of the Stock Transfer Act 1963. The transfer of shares is subject to payment of stamp duty at 50p for each £100 of the value of the shares transferring, that is one-half of one per cent of such value rounded up to the nearest 50p. As a result, prior to the transfer being registered by the company, the Stock Transfer Form will require to be stamped with the appropriate duty. Where subscriber shares are being transferred and the value of the shares is a nominal figure of perhaps £1.00, the stamp duty payable (50p) may be dealt with by the use of a pre-stamped Stock Transfer Form. In any other case, it is necessary to submit the form for stamping along with a cheque for the appropriate amount of duty. Where the consideration is not payable in cash or where there is doubt regarding the value of the shares transferring, it will be necessary to have the stamp duty payable adjudicated by the Inland Revenue. Some transfers, such as transfers by way of gift, are exempt from duty provided that an appropriate certificate is completed on the reverse of the Stock Transfer Form. Following stamping, the transfer can then be presented to the company for registration and for issue of the appropriate Share Certificate.

Although the foregoing paragraph sets out the ordinary procedure, 7.5.2
it is, as we have seen, quite common for companies to restrict the transfer of their shares. Such restrictions can be dealt with in any number of ways and may even be subject to the absolute discretion of the directors of the company. Alternatively, the Articles of Association of the company may provide that any member wishing to transfer shares in the company must first offer those shares to the existing members in proportion to their shareholdings. This matter was considered in detail in Chapter 3. For present purposes, it is sufficient to note that anyone acquiring shares in a private company should firstly ascertain that the transfer will be registered by the directors and that no existing members of the company, or indeed any third party, has any right to claim priority with regard to such a transfer.

The Transmission of Shares

Once registered as a member of a company, the shareholder holds 7.6
his shares as an asset which will form part of the shareholder's estate. In the event of the death of the shareholder, the shares will pass to his executors who may then seek to transfer them to the shareholder's successors. Likewise, on insolvency, the shares may pass to a trustee in bankruptcy or to a liquidator. In law, the executor, trustee or liquidator is then entitled to seek registration as a member of the company or to transfer the shares to a beneficiary, creditor or some third party. This will, however, be subject again to any specific provisions contained within the Articles of Association of the company.

It is, for example, common to provide that in this eventuality the executor, trustee or liquidator is deemed to have served a transfer notice upon the company which enables the other members of the company to acquire the shares in question at a price to be agreed or otherwise determined in accordance with the Articles.

Share Certificate

7.7 Following registration of the allotment or transfer of shares, the member of the company is entitled to receive a share certificate in respect of his shareholding. In terms of section 185 of the 1985 Act, a company must issue the share certificate within two months of registration of the allotment or transfer. The share certificate is then *prima facie* evidence of the shareholder's title to his shares and will normally require to be presented to the company if the shareholder wishes to transfer the whole or any part of his shareholding. As a result, share certificates are important documents which should be carefully safeguarded. Where a certificate is lost or destroyed, however, matters may require to be dealt with by the granting of an indemnity by the member to the company confirming that he will indemnify the company for any loss arising should it subsequently transpire that he was not entitled to the shares which he claims. A simple form of indemnity is included within Schedule 16.

In the case of public companies which are listed on the London Stock Exchange, the position in respect of share certificates is different. This is as a result of the introduction of CREST which is the new electronic system for the settlement of sales and purchases of UK listed securities. CREST became operational on 15 July 1996. Under CREST, shareholders have the option as to how their shareholding is to be maintained; they can either continue to hold their shares in paper certificate form or in electric form as a computer record. Quoted companies are able to make their shares and other securities eligible for CREST pursuant to the Uncertificated Securities Regulations 1995. The rationale behind CREST is that it will remove the movement of paper around the country which is required when shares or other securities are traded in paper form.

Calls on Shares and Forfeiture

7.8 Articles 12–22 of Table A, which are commonly adopted with little or no amendment, deal with calls on shares and forfeiture. A call is a formal demand issued by a company to its members requesting payment of part or the whole of any unpaid sums on the issued share capital of the company. Although technically distinguishable from an instalment payment, the two are practically identical in nature.

When a call or instalment remains unpaid the company has, as its ultimate sanction, the ability to forfeit the shares of the offending member. The procedure for forfeiture is laid down in the Articles and must be carefully adhered to. Ordinarily there is no provision for forfeiting fully paid shares. This can cause difficulties where members or their successors can no longer be traced. It is possible to make special provision for this within the Articles of Association of the company.

Classes of Shares and Rights Attaching to Shares

Although, up until now, we have generally considered only ordinary shares, it is open to companies to allot various classes of shares differing in each case as to the rights of the various class members provided that such shares are included within the authorised share capital of the company. The Companies Acts do not make any specific provision defining different classes of shares or restricting the rights which may be attached to a particular class of shares. As a result, there is considerable flexibility in the approach which may be adopted by companies and no legal restriction on the arrangements which may be made. Commonly however, shares fall into a number of fairly well-defined categories with each class of shares being generally described by reference to the nature of the rights attaching to that class of shares. Let us consider some of these in turn. 7.9

Ordinary shares

The majority of shares issued by companies are described as ordinary shares. As a rule, an ordinary shareholder will be entitled to one vote for each share held. Subject to what is stated below, the shareholder will be entitled to share in any profits which the company determines should be distributed and, on a winding-up, the shareholder will be entitled to a proportionate part of the net assets of the company, if any. 7.9.1

Preference shares

As the name implies, the preference shareholders are generally entitled to some priority over the other shareholders of the company. Most commonly, the holders of preference shares are entitled to receive a dividend on their shares prior to any other shareholder receiving a distribution. This right will, of course, be subject to the company having profits available for distribution and it being resolved that these profits should be so distributed. It may mean, however, that the preference shareholders receive their agreed dividend to the entire or partial exclusion of the other classes of shareholder. Where 7.9.2

a company has insufficient distributable profits to pay even the preference shareholders, then there will generally be provision entitling the preference shareholders to recover the shortfall in succeeding years. In this event the shares will ordinarily be described as cumulative in nature.

Traditionally, preference shareholders, while having priority with regard to distribution of profits, would receive a fixed rate of return on their shares. Preference shares might, for example be stated to be entitled to a six per cent return net of tax. While their priority gives to the preference shareholders a greater certainty of receiving their annual dividend, they are not, in these circumstances entitled to participate further in the profits of the company and any additional sums available for distribution and agreed to be distributed will fall to the ordinary shareholders. However, where preference shares have been adopted as a mechanism for the investment of venture or development capital in private companies, provision is often made for the preference shareholders to receive not only a fixed or fluctuating preferential dividend, but also a further participating dividend where additional profits are available for distribution. The basis of calculating the level of such participating dividends can be complex and may, for example be calculable by reference to turnover or profits of the company by reference to a predetermined formula.

Convertible shares

7.9.3 It is possible to provide that shares of one class may be converted to shares of another class on a predetermined basis or subject to an agreed formula. Generally, the ability to convert will apply on the occurrence of one or more specified events such as, for example, the sale of the business of the company, on a takeover or merger, or on the company's applying for listing on the London Stock Exchange. Although not directly in point, it is worth noting that similar conversion rights may be granted in relation to loans given to a company whereby the lender may convert all or part of the loan into a shareholding in the company, again on a predetermined basis. Alternatively, such rights of conversion may be exercisable at the option of one or other of the parties on a specified date or over a specified period.

Redeemable shares

7.9.4 In terms of section 159 of the Companies Act 1985, a company may, if authorised by its Articles, issue shares which are stated to be redeemable on specific terms. Again redemption may occur at the option of one or other of the parties, on the happening of a specific event, or on a specified date or dates. A redemption price will either be specified within the Articles or, alternatively, a formula fixed for determining the redemption sum. Section 159A which was inserted by section 133 of the 1989 Act stipulates a number of conditions for the issue of redeemable shares but this has yet to be brought into force.

Deferred or founder's shares

While all of the foregoing classes of shares may be seen as giving to the shareholder some additional right it is perfectly possible to defer the rights of a specific class of shares as against the ordinary or preferred shares of the company. Such shares are commonly referred to as either deferred shares or, where these have been allotted to the initial promoters of the company, as founder's shares. The basis of the deferment can be on whatever terms may be agreed between the parties. 7.9.5

Other categories

As indicated, the classes into which shares can be divided are without limitation. Sometimes shares may be divided into two separate classes perhaps identified as being 'A' ordinary shares and 'B' ordinary shares respectively although the rights attaching to each of the shares may be identical. This device may be of assistance where it is necessary to identify shares belonging to a particular shareholder or group. Where, for example a company is set up on the basis of an equal partnership between two individuals or families, it may be appropriate that the shares held by one family are separately identified from those held by the other. By this means, when preparing the transfer provisions in the Articles of Association of the company, it can be provided that any member holding 'A' ordinary shares and wishing to transfer those shares must first offer them to the other holders of 'A' ordinary shares who have an opportunity to buy these before they are then offered to the 'B' ordinary shareholders. By this means the balance between the two groups can be maintained. Further rights may be attached to each class such as the right to nominate and have appointed a director or to attend and vote on certain key matters. The voting rights attached to shares can, as we have noted previously, be varied in such manner as the parties may agree. Shares may be classified as non-voting and this is relatively common in the case of preference shares. Alternatively, the right to vote may be granted only in specified circumstances. For example, it is common to provide that preference shareholders have no vote in the ordinary case but do acquire voting rights where preferential dividends are more than six months in arrears or in various other specified circumstances. 7.9.6

Finally, as an example of the variety of types of share, reference may be made to the so-called "golden share" which was taken up by the government in relation to various company privatisations. The golden share was a single share retained by the government with provision in the Articles of Association that the consent of the holder of the golden share must first be obtained prior to various transactions taking place.

Perhaps the most intimidating aspect of share classification is the combination of one or more of the characteristics noted above in respect of a particular class of share. This is now common in certain types of equity investment by financial institutions and the like where the institution will invest money in a company in return for the allotment of cumulative convertible redeemable participating preference shares in the share capital of the company. The narration of the rights attaching to these shares may take up several pages of the Articles of Association of the company.

Purchase or Redemption by a Company of its own Shares

7.10.1 The concept of a company acquiring or redeeming its own shares was introduced by the Companies Act 1981. The statutory provisions are now to be found in Chapter VII of Part V of the Companies Act 1985.

For private companies the ability to purchase their own shares may enable a company to buy out a dissenting or disinterested minority. Equally it may enable the management of a company to buy out an investor or for a family to retain control while the company buys out the interest of one or more members of the family. This is of particular relevance where the individuals involved who are retaining an interest in the company do not have surplus cash themselves. Equally it may be useful for investors in private companies as a mechanism for enabling them to realise their investments where there is no external market for the company's shares.

The above reasons may be inappropriate in the case of a public company. The provision for issue of redeemable shares may however be useful for public companies wishing to raise medium term finance without over-weighting their loan/equity gearing in favour of loan capital. A public company can also use the purchase of shares to bring the company's share capital into line with its net asset value. This may assist in discouraging takeovers where the net asset value of a company is low relative to its share capital.

7.10.2 Chapter IV of Part V of the Companies Act 1985 contains detailed statutory provisions for a formal reduction of capital by a company. These provisions include the requirement for an application to be made to the relevant court. Suitable safeguards are provided for creditors. These provisions continue to apply even although, in terms of Chapter VII, a private company can now purchase its own shares, not only from distributable profits but also from capital. Clearly such a mechanism is also a reduction of capital and accordingly similar safeguards are included in Chapter VII of the Act. The provisions apply to fully paid shares only and, where a reduction is effected by writing off sums due on partly paid shares, this will continue to fall under the rules of Chapter IV requiring a formal reduction of capital.

The basic requirements for the purchase or redemption of shares 7.10.3
by both public and private companies are as follows:

(a) the Articles of Association must contain authority for the purchase or redemption of shares by the company;
(b) the shares must be fully paid;
(c) once purchased or redeemed these shares must be cancelled, they cannot be assigned or held by the company as an asset;
(d) the funds used in respect of the purchase or redemption must come from either distributable profits or from a fresh issue of shares and (except where a private company purchases out of capital) the capital of the company must be maintained;
(e) any premium paid on purchase or redemption must be financed out of distributable profits unless the shares themselves were issued at a premium in which case some relief is allowed.

The 1985 Act distinguishes between off-market and market purchases 7.10.4
of shares. Off-market purchases are those taking place outwith a recognised investment exchange such as the London Stock Exchange.

It includes private contracts and "over-the-counter markets". In this case a special resolution is required which must, in the case of a public company, specify a time limit on the authority granted of not more than 18 months. The resolution must specifically approve the exact terms of the contract which must be available for inspection at the registered office of the company for a period of 15 days prior to the meeting at which the resolution is to be considered. The shares to be purchased carry no vote in respect of the resolution and a member holding both shares to be purchased and shares to be retained can vote on the retained shares on a poll only.

Market purchases are less strictly controlled requiring an ordinary resolution only. The exact terms of the contract need not be stipulated although some parameters are fixed, including, in particular, the maximum number of shares to be bought and the minimum and maximum prices to be paid. Again there must be a specific time-limit for the authority, not exceeding 18 months. In this case there is no disenfranchisement of members. It should be noted, however, that the London Stock Exchange Rules for the admission of securities to listing contain further specific requirements for listed companies.

7.10.5 Where a company redeems or purchases its own shares, a note giving details of the transaction requires to be included within the accounts of the company for the relevant period. The Registrar of Companies must be notified within 28 days of the acquisition and a copy of the contract must be kept at the registered office, available for examination, for a period of 10 years.

7.10.6 A private company may, if authorised by its Articles of Association, redeem or purchase shares out of its capital. The amount of capital used is defined as the "permissible capital payment," that is the price of redemption or purchase less distributable profits or the proceeds of any fresh issue of shares. Thus all distributable profits must be utilised before any resort is made to capital. In order to calculate distributable profits, accounts are required to a date within three months of the directors' statutory declaration referred to hereafter. As a result it may be necessary to prepare an interim report on the company's financial position before proceeding with such an acquisition.

A number of specific safeguards apply with a view to protecting both the creditors of the company and the company members. These may be summarised as follows.

(a) The directors require to give a statutory declaration specifying the permissible capital payment and confirming that (i) immediately following payment the company will be able to pay its debts, and (ii) the company will be able to carry on its business and to repay its debts as they fall due within the year following such acquisition. Attached to the statutory declaration must be an auditors' report stating that, after due enquiry, the auditors can confirm that the permissible capital payment has been properly determined and that the director's declaration is a reasonable one.

(b) A special resolution is required to approve the acquisition and, as before, the shares to be purchased are disenfranchised with regard to such resolution. The special resolution must be passed on the same day or within the week following the statutory declaration, and payment must be made not earlier than five weeks and not later than seven weeks after the special resolution.

(c) Within one week of the special resolution, the company must publish details of the transaction in the *Gazette.* In addition, similar notice must be given in an appropriate national paper or written notice must be given to each and every creditor. Not later than the "first notice date," a copy of the statutory declaration and auditors' report must be registered with the Registrar of Companies.

(d) Any member who did not consent or vote in favour of the special resolution and any creditor of the company may within five weeks of the resolution apply to the court for the resolution to be cancelled. The court may confirm or cancel the resolution as it thinks fit.

(e) If, within one year following the acquisition, the company is wound up and is unable to pay its debts, the directors and any person who sold his shares to the company are liable for the debts of the company up to the amount paid out of the capital of the company in respect of the acquisition. If, however, a director can show reasonable grounds for having made the statutory declaration he may be able to avoid such liability.

No purchase or redemption by a company of its shares should be 7.10.7 carried through without first seeking advice both from the company's legal advisers and from the company's accountants. This is particularly important as the purchase of the company's shares may be treated as a distribution for tax purposes giving rise to a charge to advance corporation tax against the company. In order to avoid such tax treatment it is necessary to show that the shares being acquired fall within a number of specific criteria. In particular the following points require to be met:

(a) the shares must be held for not less than five years prior to the date of acquisition;
(b) the purchase must be shown to be for the benefit of the trade of the company;
(c) the acquisition must include the whole or substantially the whole of the relevant member's shareholding. Notwithstanding the foregoing, an acquisition may be made by a number of instalments provided that not less than one-quarter of the shareholder's holding is acquired on each occasion.

The foregoing are the key requirements of the legislation only, and, as indicated, in each case detailed tax advice should be obtained. In particular the company's accountants will ordinarily require to seek clearance from the Inland Revenue confirming that the transaction will not be treated as a distribution for tax purposes.

Financial Assistance by a Company for the Acquisition of its own Shares

Generally, in terms of section 151 of the Companies Act 1985, where 7.11.1 a person is acquiring or is proposing to acquire shares in a company, it is not lawful for the company or for any of its subsidiaries to give financial assistance directly or indirectly for the purpose of that acquisition before or at the same time as the acquisition takes place. Likewise where a person has acquired shares in a company, it is unlawful for the company or any of its subsidiaries to give financial assistance directly or indirectly for the purpose of reducing or discharging any liability incurred by the purchaser.

Financial assistance for the purpose of the statutory sections is broadly defined and includes not only the provision of loans or gifts but also the giving of any guarantee, security or indemnity.

Notwithstanding the foregoing general provisions, section 153 of the 1985 Act contains a number of specific exemptions. These may be summarised as follows.

7.11.2 A company may give financial assistance where the company's principal purpose in giving such assistance is not for the purpose of the acquisition of the shares but is incidental to some larger purpose of the company and where it can be shown that the assistance is given in good faith in the interests of the company. Payment of an institutional investor's legal costs might fall within such an exemption.

Further specific examples are:

(a) payment of dividends or the allotment of bonus shares;
(b) a reduction of capital confirmed by order of the court under section 137 of the Act or a redemption or purchase of the company's own shares;
(c) anything done in pursuance of an order of the court under section 425 of the Act (compromises and arrangements with creditors and members) or made pursuant to certain arrangements under the Insolvency Act 1986;
(d) where the lending of money is part of the ordinary business of the company, the lending of money in the course of such business is not struck at by the statutory provisions;
(e) the provision of assistance in connection with an employee share scheme for the acquisition of fully paid shares in the company is also exempt.

In the last two cases the exemptions do not apply to public companies if the provision of assistance by the company would reduce the net assets of the company or, to the extent that those assets are reduced, where the assistance is made otherwise than out of distributable profits.

7.12 In the case of private companies, section 155 of the Act provides a further exemption to the statutory prohibition provided that the procedure set forth in the Act is carefully adhered to. Assistance may only be given if the company has net assets which are not thereby reduced or, to the extent that they are reduced, if the assistance is provided out of distributable profits.

The essential features of the procedure to be adopted are as follows.

(a) A statutory declaration requires to be made by all of the directors of the company confirming particulars of the assistance to be given, of the business of the company and identifying the person to whom the assistance is to be given. The declaration, which requires to be in the prescribed statutory form, states that the directors have formed the opinion as regards the company's initial situation immediately following the date of such assistance that there will be no ground on which it could be found unable to pay its debts and, if it is intended to commence the winding-up of the company within 12 months of that date, that the company will be able to pay its debts in full within 12 months of the winding-up commencing, or in any other case that the company will be able to pay its debts as they fall due during the year immediately following the date of the assistance.

(b) The directors' statutory declaration requires to have annexed to it a report addressed to the directors by the company's auditors confirming that they have enquired into the state of affairs of the company and that they are not aware of anything to indicate that the opinion expressed by the directors in the declaration as to any of the matters mentioned in the declaration is unreasonable in all the circumstances.

(c) The statutory declaration and auditor's report must be registered with the Registrar of Companies together with a copy of any special resolution passed by the company as undernoted.

(d) A special resolution is then required approving the giving of the financial assistance. The resolution must be passed on the date on which the directors make the required statutory declaration or within the week immediately following that date.

(e) Where a resolution has been passed an application may be made to the court for cancellation of the resolution by the holders of not less than 10 per cent in aggregate of the nominal value of the company's issued share capital or any class of it or, if the company is not limited by shares, by not less than 10 per cent of the company's members.

(f) Following the passing of the special resolution, the company is then enabled to carry through the financial assistance. Such assistance shall not be given before the expiry of the period of four weeks beginning with the date on which the special resolution is passed (unless every member who voted was in favour of the resolution) or, where application is made to court, as noted above, until the final determination of such application has been issued. The assistance shall not be given after the expiry of eight weeks beginning with the date on which the directors gave the required statutory declaration.

The statutory provisions relating to financial assistance for the purchase of a company's own shares have given rise to many problems of interpretation. Lawyers have often interpreted the sections literally without regard to the purpose of the legislation. The result has been that many transactions are believed by lawyers to be potentially caught by the sections even although this was probably never intended. The government has been reviewing the statutory provisions and it is thought that amending legislation may be brought in at some future date to try and clarify the rules. In the meantime, as stated, professional advice should always be sought if you are contemplating any such transaction.

Chapter 8

CHANGES TO COMPANY STRUCTURE

Change of Name

8.1 As indicated in Chapter 3, a company may alter its name by special resolution in terms of section 28 of the Companies Act 1985. Where a company has been registered with a name which appears to the Secretary of State to be too similar to a name already appearing on the register then the Secretary of State may order the company to amend its name within 12 months of its original registration. Furthermore, if it appears to the Secretary of State that misleading information has been given for the purposes of a company's registration with a particular name or that undertakings or assurances have been given for that purpose and have not been fulfilled, he may within five years of the date of such registration direct the company to amend its name. This might arise where, for example, a company has been incorporated with the word "Holdings" as part of its name on the basis of an assurance by the directors or promoters of the company that the company would have one or more subsidiaries. Where it subsequently transpires that the company does not acquire any such subsidiaries, then the Secretary of State might exercise his powers under the Act to order the amendment of the company's name.

Where a company changes its name, a certified copy of the relevant resolution must be submitted to the Registrar of Companies who, if satisfied with the name chosen, will issue a Certificate of Incorporation on Change of Name similar in form to the original Certificate of Incorporation for the company. The company's registered number remains unaltered. It is important to note that the change of name takes effect only from the date of the Certificate of Incorporation on Change of Name and is ineffective prior to that date. This can give rise to some problems in practice where a company is trading and where the date of the change is significant, perhaps marking the date of a takeover or similar event. In these circumstances it is clearly essential to ensure that there is no delay in registration of the appropriate resolution and it may be appropriate to use the expedited procedure allowing the change to be made on the day of application.

Sometimes, and particularly where one company takes over the business and assets of another, companies may wish to swop names. There is no legal reason why this cannot be carried through, but to avoid any problems arising with regard to the companies having the same name at any one time it is recommended that the appropriate resolution for each company be submitted together with a covering letter to the registrar.

Along with the certified copy resolution, it is necessary, when altering a company name, to submit to the Registrar the registration dues payable in respect of a change of name. Currently, the sum payable is £10 or £100 for the expedited service.

Immediately upon receipt of the Certificate of Incorporation on Change of Name, this should be copied to all key parties concerned with the company including, in particular, the company's auditors and bankers. The company's notepaper, stationery and chequebooks will require to be altered forthwith and, if required, a new seal obtained. Other authorities may also require a copy of the certificate including, in particular, the Inland Revenue and H.M. Customs & Excise.

The passing of the special resolution required to change the name of the company may be dealt with either by the convening of an extraordinary general meeting, possibly on short notice, or by written resolution of the members. Forms which may be used in either case are included within Schedule 14.

Alteration of Objects

In terms of section 4 of the Companies Act 1985 as substituted by 8.2
section 110 of the Companies Act 1989, a company may by special resolution alter its Memorandum with respect to the statement of the company's objects. Formerly such alteration had to fall within certain defined categories although these were so widely drawn as to generally pose little restriction on the alterations which could be effected. Now companies are entirely free to choose whatever objects they require, provided that these are not immoral or illegal. Following the passing of the required resolution, this must again be intimated to the Registrar within 15 days. The alteration is, however, effective immediately upon its passing subject always to any objection as aforementioned.

Where a company's Memorandum has been altered by special resolution in terms of section 4 of the 1985 Act, application may be made to the court for such alteration to be cancelled by the holders of not less, in aggregate, than 15 per cent in nominal value of the company's issued share capital or any class of the company's share capital or, if the company is not limited by shares, by not less than

15 per cent of the company's members. An application for the cancellation of an alteration cannot be made by any person who has consented to or voted in favour of such alteration. The application must be made within 21 days following the passing of the resolution and, on hearing such application, the court may make an order confirming the alteration either wholly or in part and on such terms and conditions as it thinks fit. In particular, the court's order may provide for the purchase by the company of the shares of any of the members of the company and for an associated reduction in the capital of the company. Where an application to court is made, the company must forthwith give notice in the prescribed form to the Registrar of Companies and within 15 days of the relevant court order, deliver to the Registrar an office copy of the order.

Alteration of Articles

8.3 In terms of section 9 of the Companies Act 1985, subject to the provisions of the Act and to any provisions contained within the Memorandum of Association a company may by special resolution alter its Articles. Alterations so made are, again subject to the Act, as valid as if originally contained within the Articles and are subject in like manner to alteration by special resolution.

It may perhaps be usefully noted here that a member of a company cannot be bound by an alteration made to either the Memorandum or Articles of Association of the company after the date on which he became a member if or insofar as the alteration requires him to take or subscribe for more shares than the number held by him at the date on which the alteration was made, or if the alteration in any way increases his liability as at that date to contribute to the company's share capital or otherwise to pay money to the company. This provision may be waived by written agreement of the member.

Again, a point to note generally is that where a company is required to send to the Registrar any document making or evidencing an alteration to the company's Memorandum or Articles the company should also submit, along with the copy resolution, a printed copy of the Memorandum or Articles as so amended.

Alteration of capital

8.4.1 In terms of section 121 of the Companies Act 1985, a company may, if authorised by its Articles, alter the conditions of its Memorandum in any of the following ways:

(a) to increase its share capital by the creation of new shares;
(b) to consolidate and divide any of its share capital into shares of larger amounts than its existing shares;

(c) to convert all or any of its paid up shares into stock and to reconvert that stock into paid-up shares;
(d) to sub-divide its shares or any of them into shares of smaller amounts;
(e) to cancel shares which have not been taken or agreed to be taken by any person and to diminish the amount of the company's authorised share capital by the amount of the shares so cancelled.

Any of the foregoing alterations can be effected by ordinary resolution of the members of the company. It should be noted that the cancellation of authorised share capital under this section does not constitute a reduction of capital as hereinafter referred to. Any alteration in terms of the foregoing provisions must be intimated to the Registrar of Companies within one month of the relevant resolution on the prescribed form. In the case of an increase in the authorised share capital of the company, intimation must be made within 15 days of the relevant resolution stating the rights attaching to the new shares which are to be created and providing the Registrar with a copy of the relevant resolution.

Where the share capital of the company is divided into separate 8.4.2
classes, the rights attaching to each class may be altered in accordance with the provisions of Chapter II of Part V of the 1985 Act. These provisions should be studied in detail where any such alteration is proposed. In summary, however, it is generally essential to obtain a resolution of the holders of three-quarters in nominal value of the issued shares of the relevant class or an extraordinary resolution passed at a separate meeting of the holders of that class of shares. Section 127 of the Act provides for a right of objection for the holders of not less than 15 per cent of the issued shares of the relevant class and on the making of such an application, the variation is postponed until confirmed by the court. Application must be made to the court within 21 days following the relevant alteration.

Chapter IV of Part V of the Act makes provision with regard to a 8.4.3
reduction in the issued share capital of a company. Subject to the comments made in Chapter 7 regarding the purchase or redemption by a company of its own shares, any reduction in the share capital of the company requires to be carried through in accordance with the terms of this part of the Act. It is recommended that legal and accounting advice be taken prior to any such reduction. In summary, however, the requirements of the Act are as follows.

(a) Although the alteration may be made in any way, the Act makes specific reference to three methods of reduction, namely: the extinction or reduction of the liability on any issued shares which have not yet been paid up or the extinction or reduction of liability on any shares; the cancellation of any paid-up share capital which is lost or unrepresented by available assets; or by the paying off of any paid-up share capital which is in excess of the company's requirements.

(b) In order to effect the reduction this must firstly be authorised by the Articles of Association of the company and by a special resolution of the members of the company.

(c) Following the passing of the required resolution, the company must apply to the court for an order confirming the reduction. On such application any creditor of the company may object to the proposed reduction and the court must agree a list of creditors entitled to object and may make arrangements for publication of the proposed reduction. A creditor included on the list of creditors may insist either on his claim being discharged or, if the court thinks fit, may obtain security from the company to the extent of the proposed reduction.

(d) Once the court is satisfied that all creditors have either consented or have had their debts discharged or secured, the court may make an order confirming the reduction. The court order is then lodged with the Registrar of Companies at which time the reduction is then effective. Notice of such reduction is to be published in such manner as the court may direct.

Re-registration as a Public Company

8.5 Where a company has been incorporated as a private company limited by shares it can, as we have noted previously, re-register as a public company in terms of sections 43–47 of the Companies Act 1985. The Act requires first the passing of a special resolution by the members of the company agreeing to the re-registration and secondly the submission of an application for re-registration together with related documents to the Registrar of Companies.

The special resolution must (a) alter the Memorandum of Association of the company so that it states it is a public company; (b) make such other alterations to the Memorandum as may be necessary, for example changing the name of the company; and (c) make such alterations to the Articles of Association of the company as may be requisite in the circumstances.

Application must be made in the prescribed form signed by a director or the secretary of the company and must be accompanied by:

- (a) a printed copy of the altered Memorandum and Articles of Association;
- (b) a copy of a written statement from the company's auditors confirming that, in their opinion, the relevant balance sheet of the company shows that the net assets of the company were not less than the aggregate of its called up share capital and undistributable reserves;

(c) a copy of the relevant balance sheet and the unqualified auditors' report relating thereto;

(d) a copy of a valuation of any non-cash consideration received for shares recently allotted;

(e) a statutory declaration in the prescribed form confirming the passing of the required special resolution, compliance with the other statutory provisions including the minimum capital requirements set out in section 45 and that there has been no change in the company's financial position since the date of the relevant balance sheet which might have reduced the company's net assets below the sum of its paid-up share capital and undistributable reserves.

A relevant balance sheet for the purpose of the sections is prepared as at a date not more than seven months prior to the company's application for re-registration.

If satisfied with all the documents submitted to him the Registrar will issue a Certificate of Incorporation on Re-registration as a public company. The change is effective only from the date of such certificate.

CHAPTER 9

ACCOUNTS AND AUDITORS

Accounting Records

9.1 The Companies Acts provide that every company must maintain detailed accounting records disclosing with reasonable accuracy the financial position of the company at any time and enabling the directors to ensure that any balance sheet and profit and loss account prepared by the company complies with the statutory requirements. The duty to maintain accounting records is set out in detail in section 221 of the Companies Act 1985 as substituted by section 2 of the 1989 Act. The accounting records must contain entries from day-to-day of all sums of money received and expended by the company and the matters in respect of which the receipt and expenditure takes place together with a record of all assets and liabilities of the company. Where the company's business involves dealing in goods, the accounting records must also contain a statement of stock held by the company at the end of each financial year and, except in the case of goods sold by way of ordinary retail trade, a statement of all goods sold and purchased showing the goods and the buyers and sellers in sufficient detail to enable all of these to be identified.

The company's accounting records are to be maintained at its registered office or at such other place as the directors think fit and must at all times be open to inspection by the company's officers. If a company fails to comply with the requirement for maintaining accounting records then every officer of the company who is in default may be liable to a fine or imprisonment unless the officer can show that he acted honestly and that in the circumstances the default was excusable.

Preparation of Accounts

9.2 The directors of a company are under an obligation, in terms of section 226 of the 1985 Act as substituted by section 4 of the 1989 Act, to prepare for each financial year of the company a balance sheet as at the last day of the year and a profit and loss account for the year. The balance sheet is to give a true and fair view of the state of affairs of the company as at the end of the company's financial year. The profit and loss account is likewise to give a true and fair view of the profit or loss of the company for the financial year. Schedule 4 of the Act lays down detailed requirements regarding the form and content of the balance sheet and profit and loss account together with additional information to be provided by way of notes to the accounts. Compliance with the statutory form must however remain subject to the accounts giving a true and fair view and, if there are special circumstances where compliance with the statutory provisions would be inconsistent with the requirement to give a true and fair view, the directors are authorised and indeed are obliged to depart from the statutory provisions to this extent. Details of any such departure from the statutory form must be given within the accounts.

As we shall see, where a company is the parent undertaking in a group of companies the directors are obliged, as well as preparing individual accounts for their company, to prepare group accounts comprising a consolidated balance sheet showing the state of affairs of the parent company and its subsidiary undertakings together with a consolidated profit and loss account again dealing with the parent company and its subsidiary undertakings. In the case of group accounts also the overriding obligation is to give a true and fair view of the state of affairs of the group. Schedule 2 of the Companies Act 1989 inserted a new Schedule 4A to the 1985 Act setting out in detail the form and content of group accounts. Again the detailed provisions of the Schedule may be departed from if this is necessary to give a true and fair view.

Accounting Reference Date and the Company's Financial Year

As indicated, the duty to prepare accounts applies for each financial year of the company. A company's first financial year begins with the date of incorporation of the company and ends on the last day of its first accounting reference period or such other date not more than seven days before or after the end of that period as the directors may determine. Subsequent financial years begin with the day immediately following the end of the company's previous financial year and end with the last day of its next accounting reference period again subject to a seven-day discretionary period. The financial year of a company is accordingly determined by reference to the company's accounting reference period which is, in turn, determined by reference to the company's accounting reference date. 9.3

A company may, at any time before the end of the period of nine months beginning with the date of its incorporation, by notice in the prescribed form given to the Registrar, specify the date which is to be taken as its accounting reference date. The accounting reference periods of the company will then end on that date in each calendar year. Failing such notice a company's accounting reference date is, in the case of a company incorporated before April 1, 1990, March 31 in each year and in the case of a company incorporated after such date the last day of the month in which the anniversary of its incorporation falls.

A company's first accounting reference period is the period of not less than six months but not more than 18 months beginning with the date of its incorporation and ending with its accounting reference date. Subsequent account reference periods are the successive periods of 12 months beginning immediately after the end of the previous accounting reference period and ending with the accounting reference date. In terms of section 225 of the 1985 Act as substituted by section 3 of the 1989 Act, a company may amend its accounting reference date from time to time. Adjustments to the company's accounting reference date can only be made within certain parameters set out in section 225. The section and the company's accountants should be consulted prior to any such alteration being made. The accounting reference date of companies forming a group should generally be adjusted so as to be uniform throughout the group.

Subsidiary Undertakings and Group Accounts

9.4 As indicated above there may be circumstances in which a company has to prepare not only its individual accounts but also group accounts consolidating the figures both for the company itself and for any subsidiary undertakings. The terms "parent undertaking" and "subsidiary undertaking" were introduced by section 21 of the Companies Act 1989 in substitution for the former definition of a subsidiary company at least for accounting purposes.

The relationship of parent and subsidiary undertaking can arise in the following circumstances:

(a) where an undertaking holds a majority of the voting rights in another undertaking;
(b) where an undertaking is a member of another undertaking *and* has the right to appoint or remove a majority of its board of directors;
(c) where an undertaking (not necessarily a member) has the right to exercise a dominant influence over another undertaking either by virtue of provisions contained in the undertaking's Memorandum or Articles or by virtue of a control contract;
(d) where an undertaking is a member of another undertaking and controls either alone or pursuant to an agreement with other shareholders or members, a majority of the voting rights in that undertaking or;
(e) where an undertaking holds a participating interest in another undertaking and either exercises a dominant influence over it

or the parent and the subsidiary undertakings are managed on a unified basis.

The statutory provisions make it clear that a parent undertaking shall be treated as such not only in relation to immediate subsidiary undertakings but also subsidiary undertakings of those undertakings.

The effect of these definitions was to extend the definition of a group of companies for accounting purposes and accordingly to extend the obligation to prepare group accounts. The following subsidiary definitions are also of relevance.

Undertaking. Section 259 of the 1985 Act defines undertaking to include not only bodies corporate but also partnerships or unincorporated associations carrying on a trade or business whether with or without a view to profit.

Participating interest. Section 259 also defines participating interest as an interest in the shares of an undertaking held on a long term basis for the purpose of securing a contribution to the activities of the parent undertaking by the exercise of control or influence arising from or related to that interest. A holding of 20 per cent or more of the shares of an undertaking is presumed to be a participating interest unless the contrary is shown. An interest in shares is stated to include both rights of conversion and options.

Dominant influence. Paragraph 4 of Schedule 10A of the 1985 Act provides that an undertaking shall not be regarded as having the right to exercise a dominant influence over another undertaking unless it has a right to give directions with respect to the operating and financial policies of that other undertaking which its directors are obliged to comply with whether or not they are for the benefit of that other undertaking.

Control contract. Is also defined by paragraph 4 of Schedule 10A as being a contract in writing conferring a right which is of a kind authorised by the Memorandum or Articles of the Company and which is permitted by the law under which that undertaking is established.

As indicated the significance of an undertaking being held to be a subsidiary undertaking is that group accounts will then require to be prepared consolidating the accounts of the subsidiary with that of the parent. There are a number of exceptions to this requirement including, in particular, the following:

(a) where inclusion of the subsidiary undertaking is not material to the giving of a true and fair view;
(b) where the information necessary for preparing the accounts cannot be obtained without disproportionate expense or undue delay;

(c) where the parent's interest was acquired and is held exclusively with a view to subsequent resale;
(d) where the subsidiary undertaking's activities are so different to those of the parent or of the group that its inclusion would be incompatible with the obligation to give a true and fair view;
(e) in the case of small or medium-sized groups; and
(f) an undertaking is exempt from the requirement to prepare group accounts if it is itself a subsidiary undertaking whose parent is established under the law of a member of the EC and where either the company is a wholly-owned subsidiary of that parent, or where the parent holds more than one-half of the shares of the company and no request has been obtained from shareholders requiring the preparation of group accounts.

These definitions which, as stated, apply for accounting purposes only, extend the previous requirement for group accounting. The aim of the legislation with its emphasis on control rather than simply shareholding was to regulate an accounting device known as off-balance sheet financing but it may, on occasion cause difficulties for equity investors and certain joint ventures. In difficult cases, the particular circumstances of an undertaking will require to be considered with the undertaking's accountants.

It should be noted that, for anything other than accounting matters the definition of a subsidiary company, a holding company and a wholly-owned subsidiary are to be found within sections 736, 736A and 736B of the Companies Act 1985 as substituted by section 144 of the 1989 Act. Broadly speaking, in terms of the section, a company is a subsidiary of another if that other company either holds a majority of the voting rights in it or is a member of it and has the right to appoint or remove a majority of its board of directors or is a member of it and controls alone or pursuant to an agreement with other shareholders or members, a majority of the voting rights in it. The definition of subsidiary, thus turns upon voting control at general meetings of the company or the right to appoint or remove the directors of the company.

Approval, Auditing and Registration of Accounts

9.5 Once a company's accounts are prepared they require first to be approved by the board of directors. The accounts are signed on behalf of the board by a director of the company at the foot of the company's balance sheet. Prior to the amendment of section 233 of the Companies Act 1985 by section 7 of the 1989 Act, two directors were required to sign the accounts except in the case of a company with a single director. Every copy of the balance sheet which is laid before the company in general meeting or which is otherwise circulated, published or issued must state the name of the person who signed the balance sheet on behalf of the board of directors.

In terms of section 234 of the 1985 Act as substituted by section 8 of the 1989 Act, the directors require to prepare a report for each financial year of the company containing a fair review of the development of the business of the company and its subsidiary undertakings during the financial year and of their position at the end of it and stating the amount, if any, which they recommend should be paid as dividend and the amount, if any, which they propose to carry to reserves.

The directors' report must comply with the provisions of Schedule 7 to the 1985 Act as regards disclosure of the matters referred to in the Schedule. The statutory provisions should be examined carefully in preparing any directors' report. The following however is a summary of the key additional items which require to appear within the directors' report:

(a) the names of all persons who at any time during the financial year were directors of the company;
(b) the principal activities of the company and any subsidiary undertakings and any significant change in those activities during the year;
(c) any significant changes in the fixed assets of the company or of its subsidiary undertakings;
(d) details of directors' interests in shares or debentures of the company;
(e) details of any political or charitable gifts;
(f) particulars of any important events affecting the company or its subsidiary undertakings which have occurred since the end of the financial year; an indication of likely future developments in the business of the company and its subsidiary undertakings and an indication of the activities of the company and its subsidiary undertakings in the field of research and development;
(g) details regarding any acquisition by the company of its own shares;
(h) where a company employs an average of more than 250 people, details regarding the employment of disabled persons;
(i) in relation to certain companies' details regarding the arrangements in force for securing the health, safety and welfare at work of the employees of the company and its subsidiary undertakings;
(j) again where the average number of employees of the company exceeds 250, details regarding the steps taken by the company to provide employees with information, to consult with employees and to encourage their involvement in the company's affairs.

The directors' report, along with the accounts, must be approved by the board of directors and signed on behalf of the board either by a director, or by the company secretary. Again every copy of the directors' report laid before the company or otherwise circulated, published or issued requires to state the name of the person who signed the report on behalf of the board of directors.

9.6 Once the accounts and the directors' report have been prepared they must (unless exemption from audit can be obtained as noted hereafter) be audited by the auditors of the company who must append to the accounts their report confirming whether or not, in their opinion, the accounts have been properly prepared in accordance with the statutory provisions and whether or not a true and fair view is given of the state of affairs of the company. In preparing their report, the auditors must carry out such investigations as enable them to form an opinion as to whether or not proper accounting records have been kept by the company and as to whether or not the accounts are in agreement with those records. If the auditors are of the view that the accounts and accounting records are inconsistent then they must qualify their report accordingly.

9.7 The audited accounts must then be circulated to the members of the company along with any debenture holders or any other person entitled to receive notice of meetings of the company. The accounts require to be laid before the members of the company at the annual general meeting of the company called for that purpose. Following the laying of the accounts at the annual general meeting, a copy of the accounts must be lodged with the Registrar of Companies. The copy lodged must be signed by a director of the company at the foot of the balance sheet and must include the directors' and auditors' reports. In the case of a private company, the accounts for each financial year must be audited, laid before the members and lodged with the Registrar within 10 months of the end of the year. In the case of a public company the period is reduced to seven months.

Failure to meet these time limits will result in the Registrar of Companies issuing a statutory penalty notice varying with the delay involved between £100 and £1,000 in the case of a private company and £500 and £5,000 in the case of a public company.

Small and Medium-sized Companies

9.8 Although all companies must prepare full accounts for auditing and circulation to the members of the company the law has, for some time, provided that small and medium-sized companies need not register full accounts but can instead register modified accounts. The purpose behind this provision is to prevent small companies having to publicly disclose detailed provisions which might give too much information to competitors and to reduce the administrative burden. Section 247 of the 1985 Act as substituted by section 13 of the 1989 Act, sets out the qualifying conditions for small and medium-sized companies. In order to qualify a company must satisfy two or more of the following requirements:

For a small company:

1. Turnover	not more than £2.8 million
2. Balance sheet total	not more than £1.4 million
3. Number of employees	not more than 50

For a medium-sized company:

1. Turnover	not more than £11.2 million
2. Balance sheet total	not more than £5.6 million
3. Number of employees	not more than 250

The balance sheet total is defined by reference to the form of accounts included within Schedule 4 of the 1985 Act. The reference to the number of employees means the average number of persons employed by the company during the course of the year. Schedule 8 of the 1985 Act sets out the modified registration requirements for small and medium-sized companies. In summary, a small company is required only to lodge a modified balance sheet. No profit and loss account or directors' report has to be filed. In the case of a medium-sized company a full balance sheet and directors' report must be lodged, but only a modified profit and loss account is required. As full accounts must in any event be prepared by all companies for circulation to members, the value of these provisions by themselves is questionable.

Section 249 of the Act sets out a similar set of criteria for small and medium-sized groups of companies. In this case the further significance of the qualification is that small and medium-sized groups need not lodge consolidated accounts. A group will be ineligible for this exemption if any member of the group is a public company, a banking institution or insurance company or is an authorised person under the provisions of the Financial Services Act 1986. In order to meet the requirements, two or more of the following criteria must be met:

For a small group:

1. Aggregate turnover	not more than £2.8 million net (or £3.36 million gross)
2. Aggregate balance sheet total	not more than £1.4 million net (or £1.68 million gross)
3. Aggregate number of employees	not more than 50

For a medium-sized group:

1. Aggregate turnover	not more than £11.2 million net (or £13.44 million gross)

2. Aggregate balance sheet total	not more than £5.6million net (or £6.72 million gross)
3. Aggregate number of employees	not more than 250

A further relaxation of the usual statutory requirements was introduced by the Companies Act 1985 (Audit Exemption) Regulations 1994 introducing new sections 249A–249E to the Companies Act 1985. These regulations enable certain small companies to dispense with the need to have their accounts audited provided that certain criteria are met. The exemption applies only to companies with a turnover for the relevant year of less than £90,000 and a balance sheet total for that year of less than £1.4 million. Companies with a turnover of less than £350,000 (or £250,000 for a charity) which otherwise meet the exemption limits can also avoid the need for an audit if they have a report prepared by the company's accountants confirming that the company meets the statutory requirements. Section 249B of the 1985 Act provides that the exemption will be lost in a number of cases particularly where members holding 10 per cent of the nominal value of the company's share capital or, in the case of a guarantee company, 10 per cent of the members by number give notice not less than one month before the relevant year end requiring that the accounts be audited.

Dormant Companies

9.9 Where a company is dormant throughout one or more financial years it may become exempt from the requirement that auditors be appointed and that audited accounts be prepared. In order to obtain the exemption the company must pass a special resolution at a general meeting of the company confirming that the company is and has been dormant throughout the relevant period and dispensing with the appointment of auditors. Again public companies, banking or insurance companies and any company being an authorised person under the Financial Services Act 1986 are excluded from this exemption.

In terms of section 250 of the 1985 Act as substituted by section 14 of the 1989 Act, a company is deemed to be dormant during any period in which no significant accounting transaction occurs; that is no transaction which is required by section 221 of the Act to be entered in the company's accounting records. A company ceases to be dormant on the occurrence of any such transaction. Under the new provisions there is to be disregarded any transaction arising from the taking of shares in the company by a subscriber to the Memorandum in pursuance of an undertaking of his in the Memorandum.

A dormant company still requires to lodge annual accounts but these need no longer be audited and can be a fairly simple form. The form of paperwork which might be adopted in this regard is included within Schedule 15.

Annual Return

In addition to registering annual accounts companies also require to lodge, in each calendar year, an annual return in the prescribed form giving various details regarding the affairs of the company. Section 139 of the Companies Act 1989, substituting new sections 363, 364 and 365 for the 1985 Act, contains the relevant provisions. 9.10

Under the new provisions an annual return is to be delivered to the Registrar made up to a date not later than the company's "return date". The return date is either the anniversary of the company's incorporation or, if the company's last return delivered in accordance with the chapter was made up to a different date, the anniversary of that date. The return must be made within 28 days after the date to which it is made up and be signed by a director or the secretary of the company. In practice the Registrar of Companies now issues Annual Returns to every company in advance of the return date. These so called shuttle returns are completed by the Registrar from the information on the Registrar. That information should be checked, updated as appropriate and the return then resubmitted to the Registrar with the required fee.

The annual return must state the date to which it is made up and must contain the following information:

(a) the registered office of the company;
(b) the type of company and its principal business activities;
(c) the name and address of the company secretary;
(d) the name and address of every director of the company;
(e) in the case of each individual director, his nationality, date of birth, business occupation and other directorships;
(f) in the case of a corporate director any other directorships;
(g) if the Register of Members is not kept at the company's registered office, the address of the place where it is kept;
(h) if any register of debenture holders is not kept at the company's registered office, the address of the place where it is kept;
(i) if the company has elected to dispense with the laying of accounts or the holding of an annual general meeting, a statement to that effect;
(j) in the case of a company with a share capital details regarding its issued shares and the amount paid-up on those shares together with the names and addresses of every person who is a member of the company at the date of the return or who has ceased to be a member since the date of the last return.

When lodging the annual return there must also be paid a statutory fee of £15.00 in respect of such return.

Auditors

9.11 Sections 118 and the succeeding provisions of the Companies Act 1989 inserted new provisions into Chapter V of Part XI of the 1985 Act with regard to the appointment and removal of auditors and related matters. Referring to the newly-inserted sections of the 1985 Act, section 384 provides that every company is to appoint an auditor or auditors in accordance with the Act unless exempted in terms of section 388A in the case of certain small companies or dormant companies. The first auditors of the company may be appointed by the directors at any time before the first Annual General Meeting of the company and auditors so appointed shall hold office until the conclusion of that meeting. Failing appointment by the directors, the auditors of the company shall be appointed by the company in general meeting. Suitable provision is made within the Act for cases in which a private company has elected to dispense with the laying of accounts before the company in general meeting. Ordinarily, auditors hold office until the next meeting at which accounts are laid. Unless the auditors are removed or are resigning, they will normally offer themselves for re-election at such meeting. Under section 386 of the Act, a private company may elect, by elective resolution, to dispense with the obligation to appoint auditors annually, in which case, the auditors then holding office are deemed to continue in office until the company resolves otherwise. Where a company which requires to appoint auditors fails to do so, these may be appointed by the Secretary of State. The directors of the company may appoint auditors to fill a casual vacancy should this arise.

The Act sets out detailed provisions regarding the rights of auditors principally in relation to the obtaining of information and their attendance at company meetings. Remuneration of auditors is to be approved by the company in general meeting or in such manner as the company in general meeting may determine. It is common for the Annual General Meeting to resolve that the remuneration of the auditors be determined and paid by the directors of the company.

Removal of Auditors

9.12 In terms of section 391 of the 1985 Act, a company may, by ordinary resolution at any time, remove an auditor from office. Where such a resolution is passed, the company must give notice to the Registrar within 14 days in the prescribed form. Special notice procedure under section 379 of the 1985 Act is required for any resolution removing an auditor before the expiration of his term of office or appointing as an auditor a person other than a retiring auditor. The auditor whom it is proposed to remove may make written representations to the company and may request that these be notified to the members of the company.

An auditor of a company may resign his office by depositing a notice in writing to that effect at the company's registered office. The notice is ineffective unless accompanied by a statement by the auditor in terms of section 394 of the Act, which is discussed below. An effective notice of resignation brings the auditor's term of office to an end as at the date on which the notice is deposited or on such later date as may be specified in it.

Within 14 days of the deposit of an effective resignation, the company must copy such notice to the Registrar of Companies. Where a resigning auditor feels that circumstances connected with his resignation should be brought to the attention of the members or creditors of the company, he may also lodge a requisition calling for the directors to convene an Extraordinary General Meeting of the company for the purpose of receiving and considering such explanation of the circumstances as the auditor may wish to make. He may also request that the company circulate a written statement regarding his resignation.

In terms of section 394 of the 1985 Act, where an auditor ceases for any reason to hold office, he must deposit at the company's registered office a statement of any circumstances connected with his ceasing to hold office which he considers ought to be brought to the attention of the members or creditors of the company or, if he considers that there are no such circumstances, a statement that there are none. Where the statement confirms circumstances which the auditor feels should be brought to the attention of members or creditors the company must, within 14 days, send a copy of the statement to every person entitled to receive copies of the accounts or must apply to the court for an order waiving such requirement.

The 1989 Act introduced detailed provisions regarding eligibility 9.13
for appointment as company auditors. Detailed provisions in this regard are contained in sections 24 and following of the 1989 Act which are intended to secure that only persons who are properly supervised and appropriately qualified are appointed company auditors and further to secure that audits by persons so appointed are carried out properly and with integrity and with a proper degree of independence.

As we have seen, the principal duty of the auditors is to audit the annual accounts of the company and to report to members regarding these. The auditors must ensure that the accounts give a true and fair view of the company's affairs and they must make such investigations as are necessary to ensure that they are able to report accordingly. In addition to this principal duty, the auditors also fulfill a number of other statutory and non-statutory roles. For example, as we have seen, the auditors may require to give certificates for certain transactions by a company, such as where a company wishes to give financial assistance for the acquisition of its own shares. Outwith the Act itself, shareholders frequently agree that matters such as the valuation of company shares should be referred to auditors for decision. In practice, the auditors of a company generally act as accounting and taxation advisers also. Indeed, they may themselves prepare the accounts for audit although clearly this will be on the basis of information provided by the company and will be subject to approval by the directors in the usual way.

Schedule 1

EUROPEAN COMMUNITY DIRECTIVES

First Directive:	Company Registers, filing of information, *ultra vires* rule—implemented by European Communities Act 1972.
Second Directive:	Minimum Capital requirements for PLCs—implemented by Companies Act 1980.
Third Directive:	Mergers of PLCs—implemented in 1987.
Fourth Directive:	Annual Accounts requirements — implemented by Companies Act 1987.
Fifth Directive:	Board Structure for PLCs including worker participation—still to be adopted.
Sixth Directive:	Divisions of PLCs—implemented in 1987.
Seventh Directive:	Consolidated Accounts—implemented by 1989 Act.
Eighth Directive:	Qualification of Auditors—implemented by 1989 Act.
Ninth Directive:	Annual and consolidated Accounts of Credit Institutions— implemented in 1993.
Tenth Directive:	Disclosure Requirements for Major Holdings in Listed Companies— implemented in 1991.
Eleventh Directive:	Disclosure Requirements in respect of Branch offices — implemented in 1993.
Twelfth Directive:	Single Member Private Limited Companies — implemented in 1992.

Schedule 2

REGULATORY PROVISIONS AND RELEVANT BODIES

Word or Expression	*Relevant Legislation*	*Relevant Body*
Architect	Section 1, Architects Registration Act 1938	The Registrar, Architects Registration Council of the United Kingdom, 73 Hallam Street, London WlN 6EE
Credit Union	Credit Union Act 1979	The Registrar of Friendly Societies, 15/17 Great Marlborough Street, London WlV 2AX
Veterinary Surgeon, Veterinary, Vet	Sections 19/20, Veterinary Surgeons Act 1966	The Registrar, Royal College of Veterinary Surgeons, 32 Belgrave Square, London SWlX 8QP
Dentist, Dental Surgeon, Dental Practitioner	Dentists Act 1984	The Registrar, General Dental Council, 37 Wimpole Street, London WlM 8DQ
Drug, Druggist, Pharmaceutical, Pharmaceutist, Pharmacist, Pharmacy	Section 78, Medicines Act 1968	The Head of the Law Dept., The Pharmaceutical Society of Great Britain, 1 Lambeth High Street, London SEl 7JN

Optician, Ophthalmic Optician, Dispensing Optician, Enrolled Optician, Registered Optician	Sections 9 and 28, Opticians Act 1989 and Health and Social Security Act 1984	The Registrar, General Optical Council, 41 Harley Street, London WlN 3DJ
Bank, Banker, Banking Deposit	Banking Act 1979	Bank of England, Threadneedle Street, London EC2R 8AH
Red Cross	Geneva Convention Act 1957	Seek advice of Registrar
Insurance Broker, Assurance Broker, Re-Insurance Broker, Re-Assurance Broker	Sections 2 and 3, Insurance Brokers (Registration) Act 1977	The Insurance Brokers Registration Council, 15 St Helen's Place, London EC3A 6DS
Chiropodist, Dietician, Medical Laboratory Technician, Occupational Therapist, Orthoptist, Physiotherapist, Radiotherapist, Radiographer, Remedial Gymnast	Professions Supplementary to Medicine Act 1960 if preceded by "Registered", or "State Registered"	Room 12.26, Department of Health and Social Security, Hannibal House, Elephant & Castle, London SEl 6TE

SCHEDULE 3

COMPANY AND BUSINESS NAMES REGULATIONS 1981 (S.I. 1981 No. 1685)

In terms of the above regulations the use of the words and expressions in Column 1 below as part of a company's name requires the approval of the body specified in Columns 2 or 3 below:

Word or Expression	*Relevant Body For England & Wales*	*Relevant Body for Scotland*
Abortion	1	1
Apothecary	2	3
Association	4	5
Assurance	4	5
Assurer	4	5
Authority	4	5
Benevolent	4	5
Board	4	5
British	4	5
Chamber of Commerce	4	5
Chamber of Industry	4	5
Chamber of Trade	4	5
Charitable	6	7
Charity	6	7
Charter	4	5
Chartered	4	5
Chemist	4	5
Chemistry	4	5
Contact Lens	8	8
Co-operative	4	5
Council	4	5
Dental	9	9
Dentistry	9	9
District Nurse	10	10
Duke	11	12
England	4	5

English	4	5
European	4	5
Federation	4	5
Friendly Society	4	5
Foundation	4	5
Fund	4	5
Giro	4	5
Great Britain	4	5
Group	4	5
Health Centre	13	13
Health Service	14	14
Health Visitor	10	10
Her Majesty	11	12
His Majesty	11	12
Holding	4	5
Industrial and Provident Society	4	5
Institute	4	5
Institution	4	5
Insurance	4	5
Insurer	4	5
International	4	5
Ireland	4	5
Irish	4	5
King	11	12
Midwife	10	10
Midwifery	10	10
National	4	5
Nurse	10	10
Nursing	10	10
Patent	4	5
Patentee	4	5
Police	15	16
Polytechnic	17	17
Post Office	4	5
Pregnancy Termination	1	1
Prince	11	12
Princess	11	12
Queen	11	12
Reassurance	4	5
Reassurer	4	5
Register	4	5
Registered	4	5
Reinsurance	4	5
Reinsurer	4	5
Royal	11	12

Royale	11	12
Royalty	11	12
Scotland	4	5
Scottish	4	5
Sheffield	4	5
Society	4	5
Special School	18	18
Stock Exchange	4	5
Trade Union	4	5
Trust	4	5
United Kingdom	4	5
University	19	19
Wales	4	5
Welsh	4	5
Windsor	11	12

KEY

1. Department of Health, Area 423, Wellington House, 133–155 Waterloo Road, London SE1 8UG.

2. The Worshipful Society of Apothecaries of London, Apothecaries Hall, Blackfriars Lane, London EC4V 6EJ

3. The Royal Pharmaceutical Society of Great Britain, 1 Lambeth High Street, London SE1 7JN

4. The Secretary of State, per the Registrar of Companies, Companies Registration Office, Companies House, Crown Way, Maindy, Cardiff CF4 3UZ

5. The Secretary of State, per the Registrar of Companies, Companies Registration Office, 37 Castle Street, Edinburgh EH1 2EB.

6. Registration Division, Charity Commission, St. Albans House, 57–60 Haymarket, London SW1Y 4QX.

7. Inland Revenue Claims Branch, Trinity Park House, South Trinity Road, Edinburgh EH5 3SD.

8. The Registrar, General Optical Council, 41 Harley Street, London WlN 2DJ

9. The Registrar,
General Dental Council,
37 Wimpole Street,
London WlM 8DQ

10. The Registrar, UK Central
Council for Nursing,
Midwifery and Health
Visiting, 23 Portland Place,
London W1N 3JT.

11. Home Office, A Division,
Room 730,
50 Queen Anne's Gate,
London SW1H 9AT.

12. Scottish Home & Health
Department, St Andrews
House, Regent Road,
Edinburgh EH1 3DG.

13. Department of Health,
48 Carey Street,
London WC2A 2LS.

14. NHS Management
Executive, Department of
Health, Eileen House,
80–94 Newington
Causeway,
London SE1 6EF.

15. Home Office, Police
Department, Room 510,
50 Queen Anne's Gate,
London SW1H 9AT.

16. Scottish Home and Health
Department, Police
Division, Old St Andrews
House, Edinburgh
EH1 3DG.

17. Department of Education
and Science, FHE1B,
Sanctuary Buildings,
Great Smith Street,
London SW1P 3BT.

18. Department of Education,
Schools 2 Branch,
Sanctuary Buildings,
Great Smith Street,
London SW1P 3BT.

19. Privy Council Office,
68 Whitehall,
London SW1A 2AT.

Schedule 4

STYLE MEMORANDUM OF ASSOCIATION FOR COMPANY LIMITED BY SHARES

The Companies Acts 1985 and 1989

COMPANY LIMITED BY SHARES

MEMORANDUM OF ASSOCIATION

of

____

1. The Company's name is

2. The Company's Registered Office is to be situated in [England and Wales] [Scotland].

3. The Company's objects are:

(1) Primarily, but without prejudice to the other objects of the Company, to carry on, in all or any of their branches, all or any of the following trades or businesses, namely: [here insert details of main objects of company]

(2) To carry on business as manufacturers of and dealers both wholesale and retail in and storers, hirers, carriers, exporters and importers of goods and merchandise of all kinds and merchants generally and to carry on any other business which can be advantageously or conveniently carried on by the Company and which is calculated directly or indirectly to benefit the Company or to enhance the value or render profitable any of the Company's property or rights;

(3) To acquire and hold, either in name of the Company or in that of any nominee, businesses and properties of all kinds, shares, stocks, debentures, debenture stocks, bonds, notes, obligations and securities issued or guaranteed by any

company whether incorporated or not and to exercise and enforce all rights and powers conferred by or incidental to the ownership thereof and to provide managerial, executive, supervisory and consultancy services for or in relation to any company or business or property in which the Company is interested upon such terms as may be thought fit;

(4) To establish agencies and branches and appoint agents for the purpose of the Company's business in the United Kingdom and abroad and to regulate and discontinue the same;

(5) To enter into any arrangements with any government, municipal, local or other authority that may seem conducive to the attainment of any of the Company's objects and to obtain from any such authority any rights, privileges or concessions which the Company may think it desirable to obtain and to carry out, exercise and comply with any such arrangements, rights, privileges or concessions;

(6) To apply for, secure, acquire by grant, legislative enactment, assignment, transfer, purchase or otherwise, and to exercise, carry out and enjoy any charter, licence, power, authority, franchise, commission, right or privilege which any government or authority or corporation or other public body may be empowered to grant and to pay for, aid in and contribute towards carrying the same into effect and to appropriate any of the Company's shares, debentures or other securities and assets, to defray the necessary costs, charges and expenses thereof;

(7) To apply for, promote and obtain any Provisional Order or Act of Parliament to enable the Company to carry any of its objects into effect or to effect any modification of the Company's constitution and to assist in procuring improvements in the law and to oppose any Parliamentary or other proceedings which the Company may think adverse to its interest;

(8) To acquire and undertake in any way whatever the whole or any part of the trade, business, property and liabilities of any person or company carrying on any trade or business that the Company is authorised to carry on or that is analogous thereto, or possessed of property suitable for the purposes of the Company, or to acquire an interest in, amalgamate with, or enter into partnership, or any arrangement for sharing profits, union of interests, reciprocal concession, co-operation, or mutual assistance with any such person or company and to give or accept by way of consideration for any of the things aforesaid, or

property acquired or conveyed or handed over, any shares, stock, debentures, debenture stock or securities, that may be agreed on; to enter into membership of any trade union or association or federation of employers or professional association and to pay any dues, subscriptions, levies or other payments in connection therewith;

(9) To purchase, take on lease or in exchange, hire or otherwise acquire in any way whatever, any property, heritable or moveable, real or personal and to sell, let on hire, improve, develop, mortgage, dispose of, turn to account or otherwise deal with all or any of the land, property and rights of the Company;

(10) To erect, buy, lease or otherwise acquire or provide such factories, warehouses, offices and other buildings, to manufacture, furnish, fit up and erect such machinery and to construct such other works and conveniences as may be deemed necessary for the purposes of the Company or any of them, and to alter, improve, extend, add to, maintain, repair, rebuild, replace, or remove the same and generally, from time to time, to provide all requisite accommodation and facilities for the purposes of the Company;

(11) To sell, dispose of, or transfer any part or the whole of the rights, businesses, property and undertaking of the Company or any branch or part thereof in consideration of payment in cash or in shares, stocks, or in debentures or other securities of any other company, or in one or other or in all such modes of payment, or for such other consideration as may, by the Directors, be deemed proper and to promote any other company anywhere in the world for the purpose of carrying on any business which the Company is authorised to carry on, or for acquiring all or any of the property rights or liabilities of the Company, or for any other purpose which may be deemed likely to promote or advance the interests of the Company;

(12) To apply for, secure by grant, legislative enactment, assignment or transfer, purchase, hire, licence or otherwise acquire any patents, trade names, trade marks, designs, copyrights, licences, concessions and the like, or any secret or other information as to any invention, process, matter or thing which may seem capable of being used for any of the purposes of the Company, or the acquisition of which may seem calculated directly or indirectly to benefit the Company; and to use, exercise, develop or grant licences in respect thereof, or otherwise turn to account, the property and rights so acquired, or to sell and dispose of the same;

(13) To pay for any property or business or services rendered or to be rendered in shares (to be treated as either wholly or partly paid up) or in debentures or debenture stock or in loan stocks, convertible or otherwise, and partly in cash or partly in one mode and partly in others;

(14) To invest, lend or otherwise deal with the moneys of the Company on such securities or in the stock, shares, debentures, mortgages, loans or bills of government or local authorities, or public or other companies, whether in the United Kingdom or abroad, and in such manner as the Directors may from time to time determine, and to vary and realise the same and to convert accumulated reserves or revenue into capital;

(15) To borrow money on such terms as the Directors shall think fit and to give security for the payment thereof or for the performance of any other obligations or liabilities of the Company, and to guarantee and/or give security for the payment of money by or for the performance of obligations of all kinds by any person or company including without prejudice to the generality of the foregoing any company which shall at the time be the holding company of the Company or another subsidiary of such holding company or a subsidiary of the Company all as defined in section 736 of the Companies Act 1985 or any statutory amendment or re-enactment thereof for the time being in force or any company associated with the Company in business or by reason of common shareholdings or otherwise and in security of such guarantees to assign, dispone, convey, mortgage, pledge or charge the whole or any part of the undertaking, property, assets or revenue of the Company including uncalled capital;

(16) To promote any company or companies, or to place or assist in placing or guaranteeing the placing of or underwriting any shares in any company for the purpose of acquiring all or any of the property and liabilities of the Company and to form any subsidiary company, in any part of the United Kingdom or in any other part of the world, necessary or convenient for carrying out any of the objects of the Company, or which may seem, directly or indirectly, calculated to benefit the Company;

(17) To pay all the expenses of or relating to the formation, incorporation and registration of the Company or any subsidiary or associated company in any part of the world;

(18) To enter into such insurance or assurance contracts and to insure all or any of the assets of the Company against such

risks and for such sums as the Directors shall deem appropriate and to enter mutual insurance, indemnity or protection associations, to establish an insurance fund out of the profits of the Company and to insure the Company and its Directors, employees, agents and others against claims for compensation and damages by mutual insurance or otherwise and also to enter into policies of assurance assuring the Company or others against loss through death or invalidity of or accident to any Director, employee or agent of the Company;

(19) To establish and support or aid in the establishment and support of associations, institutions, funds, trusts, and conveniences calculated to benefit employees or Directors or past employees or Directors of the Company or of its predecessors in business, or the dependants or connections of any such persons; to grant pensions or gifts to Directors, ex-Directors and/or employees or their relatives and to join in any public or local subscription proposed to be raised for any charitable, religious, patriotic, political, benevolent business or other purpose;

(20) To establish and maintain or procure the establishment and maintenance of any non-contributory or contributory pension or superannuation funds for the benefit of, and give or procure the giving of donations, gratuities, pensions, allowances, benefits or emoluments to any persons who are or were at any time in the employment or service of the Company, or of any company which is a subsidiary of the Company, or which is allied to or associated with the Company or with any such subsidiary company, either by substantial common shareholdings or one or more common directors or which is the holding company of the Company, or who are or were at any time Directors or officers of the Company or of any such other company as aforesaid, or any persons in whose welfare the Company or any such other company as aforesaid is or has been interested, and the wives, widows, families and dependants of any such person, and to make payments for or towards the insurance of any such persons as aforesaid, and to do any of the matters aforesaid either alone or in conjunction with or through the holding company (if any) of the Company or in conjunction with or through any such other company as aforesaid;

(21) To remunerate, as the Directors may decide, the officers, employees and agents of the Company and others out of, or in proportion to, the returns or profits of the Company or of any particular business carried on by it or otherwise as

the Directors may deem proper and for that purpose to enter into any arrangements they may think fit;

(22) To distribute among the members in kind any property of the Company or any proceeds of sale or disposal of any property of the Company but so that no distribution amounting to a reduction of capital be made except with the sanction (if any) for the time being required by law;

(23) To cancel or accept surrender of any share or shares of any member or members for any reasons and on any terms and conditions and as and when the Directors in their absolute discretion think fit, with or without any continuing liability attaching to such member or members, and to pay up any uncalled or unpaid capital in respect of such share or shares so cancelled or surrendered, all however so far only as can be lawfully done;

(24) To do all or any of the above things as principals, agents, trustees, contractors, sub-contractors, licensees, concessionaires or otherwise and by or through trustees, agents, sub-contractors, licensees, concessionaires or otherwise and either alone or in conjunction with others and to act as agents, licensees, concessionaires, trustees, nominees or otherwise for any person or company and to undertake and perform sub-contracts and to appoint agents, attorneys or factors for the Company;

(25) To do all such things as are incidental or conducive to the attainment of the above objects or any of them; provided always that nothing herein contained shall empower the Company to carry on, save as agents for others, the business of life, accident, fire, employers' liability, industrial, motor, or other insurance business within the meaning of the Insurance Companies Act 1982 or any act amending, extending or re-enacting the same.

The objects set forth in any paragraph of this clause shall not be restrictively construed but the widest interpretation shall be given thereto and they shall not, except where the context expressly so requires, be in any way limited to or restricted by reference to or influence from any other object or objects set forth in such paragraph or from the terms of any other paragraph or by the name of the Company. None of such paragraphs or the object or objects therein specified or the powers thereby conferred shall be deemed subsidiary or ancillary to the objects or powers mentioned in any other paragraph but the Company shall have full power to exercise all or any of the powers or to achieve or to endeavour to achieve all or any of the objects conferred by and provided in any one or more of the said paragraphs. In this clause the word "company" except where used in reference to this Company shall be deemed to include any partnership or other body of persons whether corporate or unincorporate and whether domiciled in the United Kingdom or elsewhere.

4. The liability of the members is limited.

5. The Company's Share Capital is £ divided into Ordinary Shares of £1 each with power, subject to the provisions of the Companies Act 1985 or any Act amending the same, to increase or reduce the Capital to purchase the Company's own shares and to consolidate, sub-divide, or otherwise deal with the Shares forming the Capital and to convert paid-up Ordinary Shares into Stock and re-convert that Stock into paid-up Preference Shares, redeemable or irredeemable; the Shares forming the Capital (original, increased or reduced) may be divided into such shares, with such liens, preference and other special incidents and held on such terms as may be prescribed by the Company's Articles of Association for the time being, or as the Company may from time to time determine in accordance with the said Act.

WE, the subscribers to this Memorandum of Association, wish to be formed into a Company pursuant to this Memorandum; and we agree to take the number of shares shown opposite our respective names:

Names and Addresses of Subscribers	*Number of Shares taken by each Subscriber*
	1
	1
Total shares taken	2

Dated at this day of Nineteen hundred and ninety

Witness to the above signatures:

Note: Following upon the Companies (Single Member Private Limited Companies) Regulations 1992 a private limited company can be incorporated with only one subscriber to the Memorandum of Association.

SCHEDULE 5

STYLE MEMORANDUM OF ASSOCIATION FOR CHARITABLE COMPANY LIMITED BY GUARANTEE

The Companies Acts 1985 and 1989

COMPANY LIMITED BY GUARANTEE

AND NOT HAVING A SHARE CAPITAL

MEMORANDUM OF ASSOCIATION

of

____

1. The name of the Company is

2. The registered office of the Company will be situated in [England and Wales] [Scotland].

3. The objects for which the Company is established are: [here insert details of main objects of Company].

4. In furtherance of the above objects, but not otherwise, the Company is established for the following ancillary purposes:

(a) To carry on any other charitable purpose or objective which can be advantageously or conveniently carried on by the Company by way of an extension of or in association with the objects stated in Clause 3 hereof or which may be calculated directly or indirectly to advance the objectives stated in the said lastmentioned clause.

(b) To borrow and raise money for the furtherance of the objects of the Company in such manner and on such security as the Company may think fit.

(c) To raise funds and to invite and receive contributions from any person or persons whatsoever by way of subscription, donation or otherwise, and whether absolutely, conditionally or in trust provided that the Company shall not undertake any permanent trading activities in raising funds for the above mentioned charitable objects.

(d) To invest the moneys of the Company not immediately required for the furtherance of its objects in or upon such investments, securities or property as may be thought fit, subject nevertheless to such conditions (if any) and such consents (if any) as may for the time being be imposed or required by law.

(e) To purchase, take on lease or in exchange, hire or otherwise acquire or deal with any real or personal property, whether heritable or moveable, and any rights or privileges and to construct, maintain and alter any buildings or erections which the Company may think necessary for the promotion of its objects.

(f) To sell, let, mortgage, dispose of or turn to account all or any of the property or assets of the Company with a view to the furtherance of its objects.

(g) Subject to Clause 5 hereof to employ and pay such architects, surveyors, solicitors and other professional persons, workmen, clerks and other staff as are necessary for the furtherance of the objects of the Company.

(h) to make all reasonable and necessary provision for the payment of pensions and superannuation to or on behalf of employees and their widows and other dependants.

(i) to subscribe to, become a member of, or amalgamate or co-operate with any other charitable organisation, institution, society or body not formed or established for purposes of profit (whether incorporated or not and whether in Great Britain, Northern Ireland or elsewhere) whose objects are wholly or in part similar to those of the Company and which by its constitution prohibits the distribution of its income and property amongst its members to an extent at least as great as is imposed on the Company under or by virtue of Clause 5 hereof and to purchase or otherwise acquire and undertake all or part of the property, assets, liabilities and engagements as may lawfully be acquired or undertaken by the Company of any such charitable organisation, institution, society or body.

(j) To establish and support or aid the establishment and support of any charitable trusts, associations or institutions and to subscribe or guarantee money for charitable purposes in any way connected with or calculated to further any of the objects of the Company.

(k) To do all or any of the things hereinbefore authorised either alone or in conjunction with any other charitable organisation, institution, society or body with which this Company is authorised to amalgamate.

(l) To pay all or any expenses incurred in connection with the promotion, formation and incorporation of the Company.

(m) To print and publish any newspapers, periodicals, books or leaflets that the Company may think desirable for the promotion of its objects.

(n) To do all such other lawful things as are necessary for the attainment of the above objects or any of them.

PROVIDED THAT:

(i) In case the Company shall take or hold any property which may be subject to any trusts, the Company shall only deal with or invest the same in such manner as allowed by law, having regard to such trusts.

(ii) The Company shall not support with its funds any object, or endeavour to impose on or procure to be observed by its members or others any regulation, restriction or condition which, if an object of the Company, would make it a trade union.

(iii) Provided also that in relation to any property which may come into the hands of the Company as trustees under any trust (whether established by any trust deed or any scheme of court or made in pursuance of any enactment relating to educational endorsements or war charities or otherwise) nothing herein shall authorise the Company to deal therewith otherwise than in accordance with the terms of the trust and with any law relevant thereto, nor shall the incorporation of the Company affect the liability as an individual of any member of the Management Committee or Governing Body who may be a party to such dealings.

DECLARING THAT this Clause and the whole Memorandum and Articles of Association of the Company shall be read and interpreted as if there were embodied therein an overriding qualification to the effect that no expenditure of income by the Company shall be permitted for the purpose of carrying out any activities which are not wholly charitable within the meaning of section 505 of the Income and Corporation Taxes Act 1988 or of any statutory modification or amendment thereof (which meaning shall be ascribed to the word charitable wherever used in this Memorandum) and that in all cases in which activities permitted by the objects of the Company are in their nature capable of being exercised for purposes which are not charitable or only partially so, as well as for purposes which are wholly charitable, the powers contained in the objects of the Company shall be held to limit such activities to those which will not prejudice the charitable status of the Company within the statutory meaning before mentioned.

5. The income and property of the company shall be applied solely towards the promotion of its objects as set forth in this Memorandum of Association and no portion thereof shall be paid or transferred, directly or indirectly, by way of dividend, bonus or otherwise howsoever by way of profit, to members of the Company, and no member of the Management Committee or Governing Body shall be appointed to any office of the Company paid by salary or fees or receive any remuneration or other benefit in money or money's worth from the Company.

Provided that nothing herein shall prevent any payment in good faith by the Company:

(a) of reasonable and proper remuneration to any member, officer or employee of the Company (not being a member of the Management Committee or Governing Body) for any services rendered to the Company;

(b) of interest on money lent by any member of the Company or of the Management Committee or Governing Body at a reasonable and proper rate per annum not exceeding 2 per cent less than the published base lending rate of a clearing bank to be selected by the Management Committee or Governing Body;

(c) of reasonable and proper rent for premises demised or let by any member of the Company or of the Management Committee or Governing Body;

(d) of fees, remuneration or other benefit in money or money's worth to any company of which a member of the Management Committee or Governing Body may also be a member holding not more than 1/100th part of the capital of that company; and

(e) to any member of the Management Committee or Governing Body of reasonable out-of-pocket expenses.

6. The liability of the members is limited.

7. Every member of the Company undertakes to contribute to the assets of the Company, in the event of the same being wound up while he is a member, or within one year after he ceases to be a member, for payment of the debts and liabilities of the Company contracted before he ceases to be a member, and of the costs, charges and expenses of winding up, and for the adjustment of the rights of the contributories among themselves, such amount as may be required not exceeding five pounds.

8. If upon the winding-up of the Company there remains, after the satisfaction of all its debts and liabilities, any property whatsoever, the same shall not be paid to or distributed among the members of the

Company, but shall be given or transferred to some other charitable institution or institutions having objects similar to the objects of the Company, and which shall prohibit the distribution of its or their income and property to an extent at least as great as is imposed on the Company under or by virtue of Clause 5 hereof, such institution or institutions to be determined by the members of the Company at or before the time of dissolution, and if and so far as effect cannot be given to such provision, then to some other charitable object.

WE, the several persons whose names and addresses are subscribed, are desirous of being formed into a Company, in pursuance of this Memorandum of Association.

Names, addresses and descriptions of Subscribers

Dated at this day of Nineteen hundred and ninety

Witness to the above signatures:

Note: Following upon the Companies (Single Member Private Limited Companies) Regulations 1992 a private limited company can be incorporated with only one subscriber to the Memorandum of Association.

SCHEDULE 6

STYLE OBJECTS CLAUSES

General Commercial Company

To carry on for profit, directly or indirectly, whether by itself or through subsidiary, associated or allied companies or firms in the United Kingdom or elsewhere in all or any of its branches the business of a general commercial company.

Note. This clause reflects the wording of section 110 of the Companies Act 1989 which makes provision for a company to adopt the objects of a general commercial company. If adopted then, in terms of the Act, the company has power to do all such things as may be incidental or conducive to the carrying on of any trade or business.

Management Company

To carry on business as consultants or advisers on all matters relating to the administration, management and organisation of any trade, business or profession including, without prejudice to the foregoing generality, the obtaining of personnel for any trade, business or profession and advising on the means and methods of organising, extending, developing, financing, marketing or improving any trade, business or profession and to carry on business as a general commercial company.

Development Company

To carry on the business of property developers and, without prejudice to the foregoing generality, to buy, lease, sell or otherwise deal in land and property of whatever kind and to construct, maintain, improve, develop, work, control, manage or demolish land and property of whatever kind purchased or acquired by the company whether for the purposes of investment or resale and to carry on business as a general commercial company.

Farming

To carry on the businesses of agriculture and horticulture in all their branches, breeders and raisers of stock of all classes, dealers in and distributors of agricultural or horticultural stock or produce of all descriptions live or dead, fertilisers, feeding stuffs, plant, machinery, equipment, apparatus and other agricultural or horticultural requisites of all kinds and descriptions and to carry on business as a general commercial company.

Garage Proprietors

To carry on all or any of the businesses of proprietors of garages and petrol filling stations and other depots, motor engineers, sellers, servicers, repairers, fitters, furnishers, hirers and letters on hire of motor cars, motor cycles, scooters, vans, lorries and other vehicles, agents for and dealers in spares, accessories, engines, implements, tools, furnishings and supplies of every description, mechanical, aeronautical, marine, electrical and general engineers, panel beaters, painters and sprayers, machinists, smiths, welders and metal workers, coach and body builders, haulage and transport contractors, provision merchants, tobacconists, newsagents, general merchants, agents and traders and to carry on the business of a general commercial company.

Housing Association

To promote, advance, improve, maintain, operate and provide or assist in providing housing and associated amenities for persons who are in need thereof by reason of their poverty, age, infirmity, disablement or handicap (whether mental or physical) and to carry on the business of a general commercial company.

Public House

To carry on business as proprietors of public houses, hotels, refreshment rooms, licensed victuallers, wine, beer and spirit merchants, caterers for public amusements generally (including without prejudice to the foregoing generality, the operation of discotheques) and proprietors of places of amusement, recreation, sports, entertainment and instruction of all kinds, tobacco and cigar merchants, to buy, sell, manufacture, and deal in provisions and goods of all kinds which may conveniently be supplied in connection with any of the said businesses, to establish and conduct clubs and to carry on the business of a general commercial company.

Retailers

It would be possible to have a general clause for retailing but as most retailers concentrate on a particular type of goods the objects clause is commonly adjusted accordingly, *e.g.*

To carry on the business of furniture retailers and general merchants whether wholesale or retail, house furnishers and manufacturers, cabinetmakers, upholsterers, repairers and restorers of and dealers in furniture of all types including, in particular but without prejudice to the foregoing generality, floor coverings, modern and antique furniture, pictures, picture frames, prints, ornaments, household linen, toys, books and printed material, importers and exporters of the foregoing articles, furniture removers and removal contractors, auctioneers, store-keepers, warehouse keepers and keepers of restaurants, cafes and canteens and any other premises for private and public use or entertainment and to carry on business as a general commercial company.

Taking over an Existing Business

Where a company is taking over an existing business it used to be common to insert a first sub-paragraph narrating that fact, for example:

To acquire and take over as a going concern the business now carried on at under the name of together with all or any of the assets and liabilities of that business and to carry on business as a general commercial company.

This would be followed by one or more further sub-paragraphs outlining the later objects of the company after purchasing the business, as with the following:

To buy, sell, by wholesale or retail, import, export, prepare, preserve, freeze, pack, distribute and otherwise deal with food of any description including meat, game, fish, poultry, live and dead stock, fruit, dairy produce and all other consumables, preserved or otherwise and any other commodities, articles, goods or things usually or which may be conveniently dealt with in the course of carrying on the business above referred to.

The use of the preliminary paragraph dealing with the business acquisition is not legally necessary and often gives the Memorandum a somewhat archaic appearance when referred to in later years.

Transport Company

To carry on all or any of the businesses of proprietors, operators, hirers and letters on hire of and dealers in motor coaches, buses, lorries, vans, wagons, cars and any other vehicles or other mode of transport appropriate for the conveyance of passengers and goods of all kinds, organisers and conductors of coach, bus and other vehicular journeys, excursions, trips, tours and the like, transport, travel and tourist agents and specialists, proprietors and operators of taxi-cabs and car hire services, carriers, transport, haulage and cartage contractors, designers, builders, constructors and repairers of motor coaches, buses, lorries, vans, wagons, cars and any other vehicles, operators of approved Department of Trade and Industry car and public service vehicle testing stations, taxi-cab testing, agents for the sale, purchase, exchange or hire of, and dealers in vehicles, fuel, vehicle parts and conveyances of every description, mechanical and electrical engineers, proprietors of garages, repairing and other depots, proprietors and letters on hire of caravan and camping sites and all accommodation and conveniences required in connection therewith, the use of property and buses for advertising, proprietors of staff and other canteens and restaurants and shops for the display and sale of goods, articles and services relating to the operations of the Company general merchants, agents, factors and traders and to carry on business as a general commercial company.

Trustee Company

To undertake the office and carry out the duties of and act as trustee, executor, administrator, factor, attorney, manager, director, secretary, registrar, agent or nominee of and for, and to hold property, heritable or moveable, real or personal of whatever description of any other corporation, association or other body; and to undertake, perform, administer, factor and discharge any trusts, public or private, *inter vivos* or *mortis causa* and to carry on business as a general commercial company.

SCHEDULE 7

TABLE A

REGULATIONS FOR MANAGEMENT OF A COMPANY LIMITED BY SHARES

Interpretation

1. In these regulations:

"the Act" means the Companies Act 1985 including any statutory modification or re-enactment thereof for the time being in force.

"the articles" means the articles of the company.

"clear days" in relation to the period of a notice means that period excluding the day when the notice is given or deemed to be given and the day for which it is given or on which it is to take effect.

"executed" includes any mode of execution.

"office'' means the registered office of the company.

"the holder" in relation to shares means the member whose name is entered in the register of members as the holder of the shares.

"the seal" means the common seal of the company.

"secretary" means the secretary of the company or any other person appointed to perform the duties of the secretary of the company, including a joint, assistant or deputy secretary.

"the United Kingdom" means Great Britain and Northern Ireland.

Unless the context otherwise requires, words or expressions contained in these regulations bear the same meaning as in the Act but excluding any statutory modification thereof not in force when these regulations become binding on the company.

Share Capital

2. Subject to the provisions of the Act and without prejudice to any rights attached to any existing shares, any share may be issued with such rights or restrictions as the company may by ordinary resolution determine.

3. Subject to the provisions of the Act, shares may be issued which are to be redeemed or are to be liable to be redeemed at the option

of the company or the holder on such terms and in such manner as may be provided by the articles.

4. The company may exercise the powers of paying commissions conferred by the Act. Subject to the provisions of the Act, any such commission may be satisfied by the payment of cash or by the allotment of full or partly paid shares or partly in one way and partly in the other.

5. Except as required by law, no person shall be recognised by the company as holding any share upon any trust and (except as otherwise provided by the articles or by law) the company shall not be bound by or recognise any interest in any share except an absolute right to the entirety thereof in the holder.

Share Certificates

6. Every member, upon becoming the holder of any shares, shall be entitled without payment to one certificate for all the shares of each class held by him (and, upon transferring a part of his holding of shares of any class, to a certificate for the balance of such holding) or several certificates each for one or more of his shares upon payment for every certificate after the first of such reasonable sum as the directors may determine. Every certificate shall be sealed with the seal and shall specify the number, class and distinguishing numbers (if any) of the shares to which it relates and the amount or respective amounts paid up thereon. The company shall not be bound to issue more than one certificate for shares held jointly by several persons and delivery of a certificate to one joint holder shall be a sufficient delivery to all of them.

7. If a share certificate is defaced, worn-out, lost or destroyed, it may be renewed on such terms (if any) as to evidence and indemnity and payment of the expenses reasonably incurred by the company in investigating evidence as the directors may determine but otherwise free of charge, and (in the case of defacement or wearing-out) on delivery up of the old certificate.

Lien

8. The company shall have a first and paramount lien on every share (not being a fully paid share) for all moneys (whether presently payable or not) payable at a fixed time or called in respect of that share. The directors may at any time declare any share to be wholly or in part exempt from the provisions of this regulation. The company's lien on a share shall extend to any amount payable in respect of it.

9. The company may sell in such manner as the directors determine any shares on which the company has a lien if a sum in respect of

which the lien exists is presently payable and is not paid within 14 clear days after notice has been given to the holder of the share or to the person entitled to it in consequence of the death or bankruptcy of the holder, demanding payment and stating that if the notice is not complied with the shares may be sold.

10. To give effect to a sale the directors may authorise some person to execute an instrument of transfer of the shares sold to, or in accordance with the directions of, the purchaser. The title of the transferee to the shares shall not be affected by any irregularity in or invalidity of the proceedings in reference to the sale.

11. The net proceeds of the sale, after payment of the costs, shall be applied in payment of so much of the sum for which the lien exists as is presently payable, and any residue shall (upon surrender to the company for cancellation of the certificate for the shares sold and subject to a like lien for any moneys not presently payable as existed upon the shares before the sale) be paid to the person entitled to the shares at the date of the sale.

Calls on Shares and Forfeiture

12. Subject to the terms of allotment, the directors may make calls upon the members in respect of any moneys unpaid on their shares (whether in respect of nominal value or premium) and each member shall (subject to receiving at least 14 clear days' notice specifying when and where payment is to be made) pay to the company as required by the notice the amount called on his shares. A call may be required to be paid by instalments. A call may, before receipt by the company of any sum due thereunder, be revoked in whole or part and payment of a call may be postponed in whole or part. A person upon whom a call is made shall remain liable for calls made upon him notwithstanding the subsequent transfer of the shares in respect whereof the call was made.

13. A call shall be deemed to have been made at the time when the resolution of the directors authorising the call was passed.

14. The joint holders of a share shall be jointly and severally liable to pay all calls in respect thereof.

15. If a call remains unpaid after it has become due and payable the person from whom it is due and payable shall pay interest on the amount unpaid from the day it became due and payable until it is paid at the rate fixed by the terms of allotment of the share or in the notice of the call or, if no rate is fixed, at the appropriate rate (as defined by the Act) but the directors may waive payment of the interest wholly or in part.

16. An amount payable in respect of a share on allotment or at any fixed date, whether in respect of nominal value or premium or as an

instalment of a call, shall be deemed to be a call and if it is not paid the provisions of the articles shall apply as if that amount had become due and payable by virtue of a call.

17. Subject to the terms of allotment, the directors may make arrangements on the issue of shares for a difference between the holders in the amount and times of payment of calls on their shares.

18. If a call remains unpaid after it has become due and payable the directors may give to the person from whom it is due not less than 14 clear days' notice requiring payment of the amount unpaid together with any interest which may have accrued. The notice shall name the place where payment is to be made and shall state that if the notice is not complied with the shares in respect of which the call was made will be liable to be forfeited.

19. If the notice is not complied with any share in respect of which it was given may, before the payment required by the notice has been made, be forfeited by a resolution of the directors and the forfeiture shall include all dividends or other moneys payable in respect of the forfeited shares and not paid before the forfeiture.

20. Subject to the provisions of the Act, a forfeited share may be sold, re-allotted or otherwise disposed of on such terms and in such manner as the directors determine either to the person who was before the forfeiture the holder or to any other person and at any time before sale, re-allotment or other disposition, the forfeiture may be cancelled on such terms as the directors think fit. Where for the purposes of its disposal a forfeited share is to be transferred to any person the directors may authorise some person to execute an instrument of transfer of the share to that person.

21. A person any of whose shares have been forfeited shall cease to be a member in respect of them and shall surrender to the company for cancellation the certificate for the shares forfeited but shall remain liable to the company for all moneys which at the date of forfeiture were presently payable by him to the company in respect of those shares with interest at the rate at which interest was payable on those moneys before the forfeiture or, if no interest was so payable, at the appropriate rate (as defined in the Act) from the date of forfeiture until payment but the directors may waive payment wholly or in part or enforce payment without any allowance for the value of the shares at the time of forfeiture or for any consideration received on their disposal.

22. A statutory declaration by a director or the secretary that a share has been forfeited on a specified date shall be conclusive evidence of the facts stated in it as against all persons claiming to be entitled to the share and the declaration shall (subject to the execution of an instrument of transfer if necessary) constitute a good title to the share and the person to whom the share is disposed of shall not

be bound to see to the application of the consideration, if any, nor shall his title to the share be affected by any irregularity in or invalidity of the proceedings in reference to the forfeiture or disposal of the share.

Transfer of Shares

23. The instrument of transfer of a share may be in any usual form or in any other form which the directors may approve and shall be executed by or on behalf of the transferor and, unless the share is fully paid, by or on behalf of the transferee.

24. The directors may refuse to register the transfer of a share which is not fully paid to a person of whom they do not approve and they may refuse to register the transfer of a share on which the company has a lien. They may also refuse to register a transfer unless:

(a) it is lodged at the office or at such other place as the directors may appoint and is accompanied by the certificate for the shares to which it relates and such other evidence as the directors may reasonably require to show the right of the transferor to make the transfer;
(b) it is in respect of only one class of shares; and
(c) it is in favour of not more than four transferees.

25. If the directors refuse to register a transfer of a share, they shall within two months after the date on which the transfer was lodged with the company send to the transferee notice of the refusal.

26. The registration of transfers of shares or of transfers of any class of shares may be suspended at such times and for such periods (not exceeding 30 days in any year) as the directors may determine.

27. No fee shall be charged for the registration of any instrument of transfer or other document relating to or affecting the title to any share.

28. The company shall be entitled to retain any instrument of transfer which is registered, but any instrument of transfer which the directors refuse to register shall be returned to the person lodging it when notice of the refusal is given.

Transmission of Shares

29. If a member dies the survivor or survivors where he was a joint holder, and his personal representatives where he was a sole holder or the only survivor of joint holders, shall be the only person recognised by the company as having any title to his interest; but nothing herein contained shall release the estate of a deceased member from any liability in respect of any share which had been jointly held by him.

30. A person becoming entitled to a share in consequence of the death or bankruptcy of a member may, upon such evidence being produced as the directors may properly require, elect either to become the holder of the share or to have some person nominated by him registered as the transferee. If he elects to become the holder he shall give notice to the company to that effect. If he elects to have another person registered he shall execute an instrument of transfer of the share to that person. All the articles relating to the transfer of shares shall apply to the notice or instrument of transfer as if it were an instrument of transfer executed by the member and the death or bankruptcy of the member had not occurred.

31. A person becoming entitled to a share in consequence of the death or bankruptcy of a member shall have the rights to which he would be entitled if he were the holder of the share, except that he shall not, before being registered as the holder of the share, be entitled in respect of it to attend or vote at any meeting of the company or at any separate meeting of the holders of any class of shares in the company.

Alteration of Share Capital

32. The company may by ordinary resolution:

(a) increase its share capital by new shares of such amount as the resolution prescribes;

(b) consolidate and divide all or any of its share capital into shares of larger amount than its existing shares;

(c) subject to the provisions of the Act, sub-divide its shares, or any of them, into shares of smaller amount and the resolution may determine that, as between the shares resulting from the sub-division, any of them may have any preference or advantage as compared with the others; and

(d) cancel shares which, at the date of the passing of the resolution, have not been taken or agreed to be taken by any person and diminish the amount of its share capital by the amount of the shares so cancelled.

33. Whenever as a result of a consolidation of shares any members would become entitled to fractions of a share, the directors may, on behalf of those members, sell the shares representing the fractions for the best price reasonably obtainable to any person (including, subject to the provisions of the Act, the company) and distribute the net proceeds of sale in due proportion among those members, and the directors may authorise some person to execute an instrument of transfer of the shares to, or in accordance with the directions of, the purchaser. The transferee shall not be bound to see to the application of the purchase money nor shall his title to the shares be affected by

any irregularity in or invalidity of the proceedings in reference to the sale.

34. Subject to the provisions of the Act, the company may by special resolution reduce its share capital, any capital redemption reserve and any share premium account in any way.

Purchase of Own Shares

35. Subject to the provisions of the Act, the company may purchase its own shares (including any redeemable shares) and, if it is a private company, make a payment in respect of the redemption or purchase of its own shares otherwise than out of distributable profits of the company or the proceeds of a fresh issue of shares.

General Meetings

36. All general meetings other than annual general meetings shall be called Extraordinary General Meetings.

37. The directors may call general meetings and, on the requisition of members pursuant to the provisions of the Act, shall forthwith proceed to convene an Extraordinary General Meeting for a date not later than eight weeks after receipt of the requisition. If there are not within the United Kingdom sufficient directors to call a general meeting, any director or any member of the company may call a general meeting.

Notice of General Meetings

38. An Annual General Meeting and an Extraordinary General Meeting called for the passing of a special resolution or a resolution appointing a person as a director shall be called by at least 21 clear days' notice. All other Extraordinary General Meetings shall be called by at least 14 clear days' notice but a general meeting may be called by shorter notice if it is so agreed:

(a) in the case of an annual general meeting, by all the members entitled to attend and vote thereat; and

(b) in the case of any other meeting by a majority in number of the members having a right to attend and vote being a majority together holding not less than 95 per cent in nominal value of the shares giving that right.

The notice shall specify the time and place of the meeting and the general nature of the business to be transacted and, in the case of an annual general meeting, shall specify the meeting as such.

Subject to the provisions of the articles and to any restrictions imposed on any shares, the notice shall be given to all the members, to all persons entitled to a share in consequence of the death or bankruptcy of a member and to the directors and auditors.

39. The accidental omission to give notice of a meeting to, or the non-receipt of notice of a meeting by, any person entitled to receive notice shall not invalidate the proceedings at that meeting.

Proceedings at General Meetings

40. No business shall be transacted at any meeting unless a quorum is present. Two persons entitled to vote upon the business to be transacted, each being a member or a proxy for a member or a duly authorised representative of a corporation, shall be a quorum.

41. If such a quorum is not present within half an hour from the time appointed for the meeting, or if during a meeting such a quorum ceases to be present, the meeting shall stand adjourned to the same day in the next week at the same time and place or to such time and place as the directors may determine.

42. The chairman, if any, of the board of directors or in his absence some other director nominated by the directors shall preside as chairman of the meeting, but if neither the chairman nor such other director (if any) be present within 15 minutes after the time appointed for holding the meeting and willing to act, the directors present shall elect one of their number to be chairman and, if there is only one director present and willing to act, he shall be chairman.

43. If no director is willing to act as chairman, or if no director is present within 15 minutes after the time appointed for holding the meeting, the members present and entitled to vote shall choose one of their number to be chairman.

44. A director shall, notwithstanding that he is not a member, be entitled to attend and speak at any general meeting and at any separate meeting of the holders of any class of shares in the company.

45. The chairman may, with the consent of a meeting at which a quorum is present (and shall if so directed by the meeting), adjourn the meeting from time to time and from place to place, but no business shall be transacted at an adjourned meeting other than business which might properly have been transacted at the meeting had the adjournment not taken place. When a meeting is adjourned for 14 days or more, at least seven clear days' notice shall be given specifying the time and place of the adjourned meeting and the general nature of the business to be transacted. Otherwise it shall not be necessary to give any such notice.

46. A resolution put to the vote of a meeting shall be decided on a show of hands unless before, or on the declaration of the result of, the show of hands a poll is duly demanded. Subject to the provisions of the Act, a poll may be demanded:

(a) by the chairman; or
(b) by at least two members having the right to vote at the meeting; or
(c) by a member or members representing not less than one-tenth of the total voting rights of all the members having the right to vote at the meeting; or
(d) by a member or members holding shares conferring a right to vote at the meeting being shares on which an aggregate sum has been paid up equal to not less than one-tenth of the total sum paid up on all the shares conferring that right; and a demand by a person as proxy for a member shall be the same as a demand by the member.

47. Unless a poll is duly demanded a declaration by the Chairman that a resolution has been carried or carried unanimously, or by a particular majority, or lost, or not carried by a particular majority and an entry to that effect in the minutes of the meeting shall be conclusive evidence of the fact without proof of the number or proportion of the votes recorded in favour of or against the resolution.

48. The demand for a poll may, before the poll is taken, be withdrawn but only with the consent of the chairman and a demand so withdrawn shall not be taken to have invalidated the result of a show of hands declared before the demand was made.

49. A poll shall be taken as the chairman directs and he may appoint scrutineers (who need not be members) and fix a time and place for declaring the result of the poll. The result of the poll shall be deemed to be the resolution of the meeting at which the poll was demanded.

50. In the case of an equality of votes, whether on a show of hands or on a poll, the chairman shall be entitled to a casting vote in addition to any other vote he may have.

51. A poll demanded on the election of a chairman or on a question of adjournment shall be taken forthwith. A poll demanded on any other question shall be taken either forthwith or at such time and place as the chairman directs not being more than 30 days after the poll is demanded. The demand for a poll shall not prevent the continuance of a meeting for the transaction of any business other than the question on which the poll was demanded. If a poll is demanded before the declaration of the result of a show of hands and the demand is duly withdrawn, the meeting shall continue as if the demand had not been made.

52. No notice need be given of a poll not taken forthwith if the time and place at which it is to be taken are announced at the meeting at which it is demanded. In any other case at least seven clear days' notice shall be given specifying the time and place at which the poll is to be taken.

53. A resolution in writing executed by or on behalf of each member who would be entitled to vote upon it if it had been proposed at a general meeting at which he was present shall be as effectual as if it had been passed at a general meeting duly convened and held and may consist of several instruments in the like form each executed by or on behalf of one or more members.

Votes of Members

54. Subject to any rights or restrictions attached to any shares, on a show of hands every member who (being an individual) is present in person or (being a corporation) is present by a duly authorised representative, not being himself a member entitled to a vote, shall have one vote and on a poll every member shall have one vote for every share of which he is the holder.

55. In the case of joint holders the vote of the senior who tenders a vote, whether in person or by proxy, shall be accepted to the exclusion of the votes of the other joint holders; and seniority shall be determined by the order in which the names of the holders stand in the register of members.

56. A member in respect of whom an order has been made by any court having jurisdiction (whether in the United Kingdom or elsewhere) in matters concerning mental disorder may vote, whether on a show of hands or on a poll, by his receiver, curator bonis or other person authorised in that behalf appointed by that court, and any such receiver, curator bonis or other person may, on a poll, vote by proxy. Evidence to the satisfaction of the directors of the authority of the person claiming to exercise the right to vote shall be deposited at the office, or at such other place as is specified in accordance with the articles for the deposit of instruments of proxy, not less than 48 hours before the time appointed for holding the meeting or adjourned meeting at which the right to vote is to be exercised and in default the right to vote shall not be exercisable.

57. No member shall vote at any general meeting or at any separate meeting of the holders of any class of shares in the company, either in person or by proxy, in respect of any share held by him unless all moneys presently payable by him in respect of that share have been paid.

58. No objection shall be raised to the qualification of any voter except at the meeting or adjourned meeting at which the vote objected to is tendered, and every vote not disallowed at the meeting shall be valid. Any objection made in due time shall be referred to the chairman whose decision shall be final and conclusive.

59. On a poll votes may be given either personally or by proxy. A member may appoint more than one proxy to attend on the same occasion.

60. An instrument appointing a proxy shall be in writing, executed by or on behalf of the appointer and shall be in the following form (or in a form as near thereto as circumstances allow or in any other form which is usual or which the directors may approve):

"PLC/Limited

I/We, , of , being a member/members of the above-named company, hereby appoint of , or failing him, of , as my/our proxy to vote in my/our name[s] and on my/our behalf at the annual/extraordinary general meeting of the company to be held on 19 , and at any adjournment thereof.

Signed on 19 ."

61. Where it is desired to afford members an opportunity of instructing the proxy how he shall act the instrument appointing a proxy shall be in the following form (or in a form as near thereto as circumstances allow or in any other form which is usual or which the directors may approve):

"PLC/Limited

I/We, , of , being a member/members of the above-named company, hereby appoint of , or failing him, of , as my/our proxy to vote in my/our name[s] and on my/our behalf at the annual/extraordinary general meeting of the company to be held on 19 , and at any adjournment thereof.

This form is to be used in respect of the resolutions mentioned below as follows:

Resolution No. 1 *for *against

Resolution No. 2 *for *against

*Strike out whichever is not desired.

Unless otherwise instructed, the proxy may vote as he thinks fit or abstain from voting.

Signed this day of 19 ."

62. The instrument appointing a proxy and any authority under which it is executed or a copy of such authority certified notarially or in some other way approved by the directors may:

(a) be deposited at the office or at such other place within the United Kingdom as is specified in the notice convening the meeting or in any instrument of proxy sent out by the company in relation to the meeting not less than 48 hours before the time for holding the meeting or adjourned meeting at which the person named in the instrument proposes to vote; or

(b) in the case of a poll taken more than 48 hours after it is demanded, be deposited as aforesaid after the poll has been demanded and not less than 24 hours before the time appointed for the taking of the poll; or

(c) where the poll is not taken forthwith but is taken not more than 48 hours after it was demanded, be delivered at the meeting at which the poll was demanded to the chairman or to the secretary or to any director;

and an instrument of proxy which is not deposited or delivered in a manner so permitted shall be invalid.

63. A vote given or poll demanded by proxy or by the duly authorised representative of a corporation shall be valid notwithstanding the previous determination of the authority of the person voting or demanding a poll unless notice of the determination was received by the company at the offfice or at such other place at which the instrument of proxy was duly deposited before the commencement of the meeting or adjourned meeting at which the vote is given or the poll demanded or (in the case of a poll taken otherwise than on the same day as the meeting or adjourned meeting) the time appointed for taking the poll.

Number of Directors

64. Unless otherwise determined by ordinary resolution, the number of directors (other than alternate directors) shall not be subject to any maximum but shall be not less than two.

Alternate Directors

65. Any director (other than an alternate director) may appoint any other director, or any other person approved by resolution of the directors and willing to act, to be an alternate director and may remove from office an alternate director so appointed by him.

66. An alternate director shall be entitled to receive notice of all meetings of directors and of all meetings of committees of directors of which his appointor is a member, to attend and vote at any such meeting at which the director appointing him is not personally present, and generally to perform all the functions of his appointor as a director in his absence but shall not be entitled to receive any

remuneration from the company for his services as an alternate director. But it shall not be necessary to give notice of such a meeting to an alternate director who is absent from the United Kingdom.

67. An alternate director shall cease to be an alternate director if his appointor ceases to be a director; but, if a director retires by rotation or otherwise but is reappointed or deemed to have been reappointed at the meeting at which he retires, any appointment of an alternate director made by him which was in force immediately prior to his retirement shall continue after his reappointment.

68. Any appointment or removal of an alternate director shall be by notice to the company signed by the director making or revoking the appointment or in any other manner approved by the directors.

69. Save as otherwise provided in the articles, an alternate director shall be deemed for all purposes to be a director and shall alone be responsible for his own acts and defaults and he shall not be deemed to be the agent of the director appointing him.

Power of Directors

70. Subject to the provisions of the Act, the Memorandum and the Articles and to any directions given by special resolution, the business of the company shall be managed by the directors who may exercise all the powers of the company. No alteration of the Memorandum or Articles and no such direction shall invalidate any prior act of the directors which would have been valid if that alteration had not been made or that direction had not been given. The powers given by this regulation shall not be limited by any special power given to the directors by the Articles and a meeting of directors at which a quorum is present may exercise all powers exercisable by the directors.

71. The directors may, by power of attorney or otherwise, appoint any person to be the agent of the company for such purposes and on such conditions as they determine, including authority for the agent to delegate all or any of his powers.

Delegation of Directors' Powers

72. The directors may delegate any of their powers to any committee consisting of one or more directors. They may also delegate to any managing director or any director holding any other executive office such of their powers as they consider desirable to be exercised by him. Any such delegation may be made subject to any conditions the directors may impose, and either collaterally with or to the exclusion of their own powers and may be revoked or altered. Subject to any such conditions, the proceedings of a committee with two or more

members shall be governed by the Articles regulating the proceedings of directors so far as they are capable of applying.

Appointment and Retirement of Directors

73. At the first Annual General Meeting all the directors shall retire from office, and at every subsequent Annual General Meeting one-third of the directors who are subject to retirement by rotation or, if their number is not three or a multiple of three, the number nearest to one-third shall retire from office; but, if there is only one director who is subject to retirement by rotation, he shall retire.

74. Subject to the provisions of the Act, the directors to retire by rotation shall be those who have been longest in office since their last appointment or reappointment, but as between persons who became or were last reappointed directors on the same day those to retire shall (unless they otherwise agree among themselves) be determined by lot.

75. If the company, at the meeting at which a director retires by rotation, does not fill the vacancy the retiring director shall, if willing to act, be deemed to have been reappointed unless at the meeting it is resolved not to fill the vacancy or unless a resolution for the reappointment of the director is put to the meeting and lost.

76. No person other than a director retiring by rotation shall be appointed or reappointed a director at any general meeting, unless:

(a) he is recommended by the directors; or

(b) not less than 14 nor more than 35 clear days before the date appointed for the meeting notice executed by a member qualified to vote at the meeting has been given to the company of the intention to propose that person for appointment or reappointment stating the particulars which would, if he were so appointed or reappointed, be required to be included in the company's register of directors together with notice executed by that person of his willingness to be appointed or reappointed.

77. Not less than seven nor more than 28 clear days before the date appointed for holding a general meeting notice shall be given to all who are entitled to receive notice of the meeting of any person (other than a director retiring by rotation at the meeting) who is recommended by the directors for appointment or reappointment as a director at the meeting or in respect of whom notice has been duly given to the company of the intention to propose him at the meeting for appointment or reappointment as a director. The notice shall give the particulars of that person which would, if he were so

appointed or reappointed, be required to be included in the company's Register of Directors.

78. Subject as aforesaid, the company may by ordinary resolution appoint a person who is willing to act to be a director either to fill a vacancy or as an additional director and may also determine the rotation in which any additional directors are to retire.

79. The directors may appoint a person who is willing to act to be a director, either to fill a vacancy or as an additional director, provided that the appointment does not cause the number of directors to exceed any number fixed by or in accordance with the articles as the maximum number of directors. A director so appointed shall hold office only until the next following Annual General Meeting and shall not be taken into account in determining the directors who are to retire by rotation at the meeting. If not reappointed at such Annual General Meeting, he shall vacate office at the conclusion thereof.

80. Subject as aforesaid, a director who retires at an Annual General Meeting may, if willing to act, be reappointed. If he is not reappointed, he shall retain office until the meeting appoints some one in his place, or if it does not do so, until the end of the meeting.

Disqualification and Removal of Directors

81. The office of a director shall be vacated if:

(a) he ceases to be a director by virtue of any provision of the Act or he becomes prohibited by law from being a director; or

(b) he becomes bankrupt or makes any arrangement or composition with his creditors generally; or

(c) he is, or may be, suffering from mental disorder, and either:

  (i) he is admitted to hospital in pursuance of an application for admission for treatment under the Mental Health Act 1983 or, in Scotland, an application for admission under the Mental Health (Scotland) Act 1960; or

  (ii) an order is made by a court having jurisdiction (whether in the United Kingdom or elsewhere) in matters concerning mental disorder for his detention or for the appointment of a receiver, curator bonis or other person to exercise powers with respect to his property or affairs; or

(d) he resigns his office by notice to the company; or

(e) he shall for more than six consecutive months have been absent without permission of the directors from meetings of directors held during that period and the directors resolve that his office be vacated.

Remuneration of Directors

82. The directors shall be entitled to such remuneration as the company may by ordinary resolution determine and, unless the resolution provides otherwise, the remuneration shall be deemed to accrue from day to day.

Directors' Expenses

83. The directors may be paid all travelling, hotel, and other expenses properly incurred by them in connection with their attendance at meetings of directors or committees of directors or general meetings or separate meetings of the holders of any class of shares or of debentures of the company or otherwise in connection with the discharge of their duties.

Directors' Appointments and Interests

84. Subject to the provisions of the Act, the directors may appoint one or more of their number to the office of managing director or to any other executive office under the company and may enter into an agreement or arrangement with any director for his employment by the company or for the provision by him of any services outside the scope of the ordinary duties of the director. Any such appointment, agreement or arrangement may be made upon such terms as the directors determine and they may remunerate any such director for his services as they think fit. Any appointment of a director to an executive office shall terminate if he ceases to be a director but without prejudice to any claim to damages for breach of the contract of service between the director and the company. A managing director and a director holding any other executive office shall not be subject to retirement by rotation.

85. Subject to the provisions of the Act, and provided that he has disclosed to the directors the nature and extent of any material interest of his, a director notwithstanding his office:

(a) may be a party to, or otherwise interested in, any transaction or arrangement with the company or in which the company is otherwise interested;

(b) may be a director or other officer of, or employed by, or a party to any transaction or arrangement with, or otherwise interested in, any body corporate promoted by the company or in which the company is otherwise interested; and

(c) shall not, by reason of his office, be accountable to the company for any benefit which he derives from any such office or employment or from any such transaction or arrangement or from any interest in any such body corporate and no such transaction or arrangement shall be liable to be avoided on the ground of any such interest or benefit.

86. For the purposes of regulation 85:

(a) a general notice given to the directors that a director is to be regarded as having an interest of the nature and extent specified in the notice in any transaction or arrangement in which a specified person or class of persons is interested shall be deemed to be a disclosure that the director has an interest in any such transaction of the nature and extent so specified; and

(b) an interest of which a director has no knowledge and of which it is unreasonable to expect him to have knowledge shall not be treated as an interest of his.

Directors' Gratuities and Pensions

87. The directors may provide benefits, whether by the payment of gratuities or pensions or by insurance or otherwise, for any director who has held but no longer holds any executive office or employment with the company or with any body corporate which is or has been a subsidiary of the company or a predecessor in business of the company or of any such subsidiary, and for any member of his family (including a spouse and a former spouse) or any person who is or was dependent on him, and may (as well before as after he ceases to hold such office or employment) contribute to any fund and pay premiums for the purchase or provision of any such benefit.

Proceedings of Directors

88. Subject to the provisions of the articles, the directors may regulate their proceedings as they think fit. A director may, and the secretary at the request of a director shall, call a meeting of the directors. It shall not be necessary to give notice of a meeting to a director who is absent from the United Kingdom. Questions arising at a meeting shall be decided by a majority of votes. In the case of an equality of votes, the chairman shall have a second or casting vote. A director who is also an alternate director shall be entitled in the absence of his appointor to a separate vote on behalf of his appointor in addition to his own vote.

89. The quorum for the transaction of the business of the directors may be fixed by the directors and unless so fixed at any other number shall be two. A person who holds office only as an alternate director shall, if his appointor is not present, be counted in the quorum.

90. The continuing directors or a sole continuing director may act notwithstanding any vacancies in their number, but, if the number of directors is less than the number fixed as the quorum, the continuing directors or director may act only for the purpose of filling vacancies or of calling a general meeting.

91. The directors may appoint one of their number to be the chairman of the board of directors and may at any time remove him from that office. Unless he is unwilling to do so, the director so appointed shall preside at every meeting of directors at which he is present. But if there is no director holding that office, or if the director holding it is unwilling to preside or is not present within five minutes after the time appointed for the meeting, the directors present may appoint one of their number to be chairman of the meeting.

92. All acts done by a meeting of directors, or of a committee of directors, or by a person acting as a director shall, notwithstanding that it be afterwards discovered that there was a defect in the appointment of any director or that any of them were disqualified from holding office, or had vacated office, or were not entitled to vote, be as valid as if every such person had been duly appointed and was qualified and had continued to be a director and had been entitled to vote.

93. A resolution in writing signed by all the directors entitled to receive notice of a meeting of directors or of a committee of directors shall be as valid and effectual as if it had been passed at a meeting of directors or (as the case may be) a committee of directors duly convened and held and may consist of several documents in the like form each signed by one or more directors; but a resolution signed by an alternate director need not also be signed by his appointor and, if it is signed by a director who has appointed an alternate director, it need not be signed by the alternate director in that capacity.

94. Save as otherwise provided by the articles, a director shall not vote at a meeting of directors or of a committee of directors on any resolution concerning a matter in which he has, directly or indirectly, an interest or duty which is material and which conflicts or may conflict with the interests of the company unless his interest or duty arises only because the case falls within one or more of the following paragraphs:

(a) the resolution relates to the giving to him of a guarantee, security, or indemnity in respect of money lent to, or an obligation incurred by him for the benefit of, the company or any of its subsidiaries;

(b) the resolution relates to the giving to a third party of a guarantee, security, or indemnity in respect of an obligation of the company or any of its subsidiaries for which the director has assumed responsibility in whole or part and whether alone or jointly with others under a guarantee or indemnity or by the giving of security;

(c) his interest arises by virtue of his subscribing or agreeing to subscribe for any shares, debentures or other securities of the company or any of its subsidiaries, or by virtue of his being, or intending to become, a participant in the underwriting or sub-underwriting of an offer of any such shares, debentures, or other securities by the company or any of its subsidiaries for subscription, purchase or exchange;

(d) the resolution relates in any way to a retirement benefit scheme which has been approved, or is conditional upon approval, by the board of Inland Revenue for taxation purposes.

For the purposes of this regulation, an interest of a person who is, for any purpose of the Act (excluding any statutory modification thereof not in force when this regulation becomes binding on the company), connected with a director shall be treated as an interest of the director and, in relation to an alternate director, an interest of his appointor shall be treated as an interest of the alternate director without prejudice to any interest which the alternate director has otherwise.

95. A director shall not be counted in the quorum present at a meeting in relation to a resolution on which he is not entitled to vote.

96. The company may by ordinary resolution suspend or relax to any extent, either generally or in respect of any particular matter, any provision of the articles prohibiting a director from voting at a meeting of directors or of a committee of directors.

97. Where proposals are under consideration concerning the appointment of two or more directors to offices or employments with the company or any body corporate in which the company is interested the proposals may be divided and considered in relation to each director separately and (provided he is not for another reason precluded from voting) each of the directors concerned shall be entitled to vote and be counted in the quorum in respect of each resolution except that concerning his own appointment.

98. If a question arises at a meeting of directors or of a committee of directors as to the right of a director to vote, the question may, before the conclusion of the meeting, be referred to the chairman of the meeting and his ruling in relation to any director other than himself shall be final and conclusive.

Secretary

99. Subject to the provisions of the Act, the secretary shall be appointed by the directors for such term, at such remuneration and upon such conditions as they may think fit; and any secretary so appointed may be removed by them.

Minutes

100. The directors shall cause minutes to be made in books kept for the purpose:

(a) of all appointments of officers made by the directors; and
(b) of all proceedings at meetings of the company, of the holders of any class of shares in the company, and of the directors, and of committees of directors, including the names of the directors present at each such meeting.

The Seal

101. The seal shall only be used by the authority of the directors or of a committee of directors authorised by the directors. The directors may determine who shall sign any instrument to which the seal is affixed and unless otherwise so determined it shall be signed by a director and by the secretary or by a second director.

Dividends

102. Subject to the provisions of the Act, the company may by ordinary resolution declare dividends in accordance with the respective rights of the members, but no dividend shall exceed the amount recommended by the directors.

103. Subject to the provisions of the Act, the directors may pay interim dividends if it appears to them that they are justified by the profits of the company available for distribution. If the share capital is divided into different classes, the directors may pay interim dividends on shares which confer deferred or non-preferred rights with regard to dividend as well as on shares which confer preferential rights with regard to dividend, but no interim dividend shall be paid on shares carrying deferred or non-preferred rights if, at the time of payment, any preferential dividend is in arrear. The directors may also pay at intervals settled by them any dividend payable at a fixed rate if it appears to them that the profits available for distribution justify the payment. Provided the directors act in good faith they shall not incur any liability to the holders of shares conferring preferred rights for any loss they may suffer by the lawful payment of an interim dividend on any shares having deferred or non-preferred rights.

104. Except as otherwise provided by the rights attached to shares, all dividends shall be declared and paid according to the amounts paid up on the shares on which the dividend is paid. All dividends shall be apportioned and paid proportionately to the amounts paid up on the shares during any portion or portions of the period in respect of which the dividend is paid; but, if any share is issued on

terms providing that it shall rank for dividend as from a particular date, that share shall rank for dividend accordingly.

105. A general meeting declaring a dividend may, upon the recommendation of the directors, direct that it shall be satisfied wholly or partly by the distribution of assets and, where any difficulty arises in regard to the distribution, the directors may determine that cash shall be paid to any member upon the footing of the value so fixed in order to adjust the rights of members and may vest any assets in trustees.

106. Any dividend or other moneys payable in respect of a share may be paid by cheque sent by post to the registered address of the person entitled or, if two or more persons are the holders of the share or are jointly entitled to it by reason of the death or bankruptcy of the holder, to the registered address of that one of those persons who is first named in the register of members or to such person and to such address as the person or persons entitled may in writing direct. Every cheque shall be made payable to the order of the person or persons entitled or to such other person as the person or persons entitled may in writing direct and payment of the cheque shall be a good discharge to the company. Any joint holder or other person jointly entitled to a share as aforesaid may give receipts for any dividend or other moneys payable in respect of the share.

107. No dividend or other moneys payable in respect of a share shall bear interest against the company unless otherwise provided by the rights attached to the share.

108. Any dividend which has remained unclaimed for 12 years from the date when it became due for payment shall, if the directors so resolve, be forfeited and cease to remain owing by the company.

Accounts

109. No member shall (as such) have any right of inspecting any accounting records or other book or document of the company except as conferred by statute or authorised by the directors or by ordinary resolution of the company.

Capitalisation of Profits

110. The directors may with the authority of an ordinary resolution of the company:

(a) subject as hereinafter provided, resolve to capitalise any undivided profits of the company not required for paying any preferential dividend (whether or not they are available for distribution) or any sum standing to the credit of the company's share premium account or capital redemption reserve;

(b) appropriate the sum resolved to be capitalised to the members who would have been entitled to it if it were distributed by way of dividend and in the same proportions and apply such sum on their behalf either in or towards paying up the amounts, if any, for the time being unpaid on any shares held by them respectively, or in paying up in full unissued shares or debentures of the company of a nominal amount equal to that sum, and allot the shares or debentures credited as fully paid to those members, or as they may direct, in those proportions, or partly in one way and partly in the other; but the share premium account, the capital redemption reserve, and any profits which are not available for distribution may, for the purposes of this regulation, only be applied in paying up unissued shares to be allotted to members credited as fully paid;

(c) make such provision by the issue of fractional certificates or by payment in cash or otherwise as they determine in the case of shares or debentures becoming distributable under this regulation in fractions; and

(d) authorise any person to enter on behalf of all the members concerned into an agreement with the company providing for the allotment to them respectively, credited as fully paid, of any shares or debentures to which they are entitled upon such capitalisation, any agreement made under such authority being binding on all such members.

Notice

111. Any notice to be given to or by any person pursuant to the articles shall be in writing except that a notice calling a meeting of the directors need not be in writing.

112. The company may give any notice to a member either personally or by sending it by post in a prepaid envelope addressed to the member at his registered address or by leaving it at that address. In the case of joint holders of a share, all notices shall be given to the joint holder whose name stands first in the register of members in respect of the joint holding and notice so given shall be sufficient notice to all the joint holders. A member whose registered address is not within the United Kingdom and who gives to the company an address within the United Kingdom at which notices may be given to him shall be entitled to have notices given to him at that address, but otherwise no such member shall be entitled to receive any notice from the company.

113. A member present, either in person or by proxy, at any meeting of the company or of the holders of any class of shares in the company

shall be deemed to have received notice of the meeting and, where requisite, of the purposes for which it was called.

114. Every person who becomes entitled to a share shall be bound by any notice in respect of that share which, before his name is entered in the register of members, has been duly given to a person from whom he derives his title.

115. Proof that an envelope containing a notice was properly addressed, prepaid and posted shall be conclusive evidence that the notice was given. A notice shall be deemed to be given at the expiration of 48 hours after the envelope containing it was posted.

116. A notice may be given by the company to the persons entitled to a share in consequence of the death or bankruptcy of a member by sending or delivering it, in any manner authorised by the articles for the giving of notice to a member, addressed to them by name, or by the title of representatives of the deceased, or trustee of the bankrupt or by any like description at the address, if any, within the United Kingdom supplied for that purpose by the persons claiming to be so entitled. Until such an address has been supplied a notice may be given in any manner in which it might have been given if the death or bankruptcy had not occurred.

Winding Up

117. If the company is wound up, the liquidator may, with the sanction of an extraordinary resolution of the company and any other sanction required by the Act, divide among the members in specie the whole or any part of the assets of the company and may, for that purpose, value any assets and determine how the division shall be carried out as between the members or different classes of members. The liquidator may, with the like sanction, vest the whole or any part of the assets in trustees upon such trusts for the benefit of the members as he with the like sanction determines, but no member shall be compelled to accept any assets upon which there is a liability.

Indemnity

118. Subject to the provisions of the Act but without prejudice to any indemnity to which a director may otherwise be entitled, every director or other officer or auditor of the company shall be indemnified out of the assets of the company against any liability incurred by him in defending any proceedings, whether civil or criminal, in which judgment is given in his favour or in which he is acquitted or in connection with any application in which relief is granted to him by the court from liability for negligence, default, breach of duty or breach of trust in relation to the affairs of the company.

SCHEDULE 8

SHORT FORM ARTICLES OF ASSOCIATION

The Companies Acts 1985 and 1989

COMPANY LIMITED BY SHARES

ARTICLES OF ASSOCIATION

of

____

Preliminary

1. The Regulations of the Company shall be those contained in Table A specified in Statutory Instrument 1985 No. 805 as amended by Statutory Instrument 1985 No. 1052 save insofar as they are excluded or modified hereby or inconsistent herewith and said Table A is hereinafter referred to as "Table A."

2. Regulations 8, 24, 59, 64, 73, 74, 75, 76, 77, 79, 80, 95 and 96 of Table A shall not apply to the Company.

Shares

3. The Share Capital of the Company is divided into   Ordinary Shares of £1 each.

4. (a) Any Shares proposed to be issued shall first be offered to the Members in proportion as nearly as may be to the number of the existing Shares held by them respectively unless the Company shall by Special Resolution otherwise direct. The offer shall be made by notice specifying the number of Shares offered and the period (being not less than 14 days) within which the offer, if not accepted, will be deemed to be declined. The offer shall further invite each Member to state in his reply the number of additional Shares (if any) in excess of his proportion which he desires to purchase and if all such Members do not accept the offer in respect of their respective

proportions in full the Shares not so accepted shall be used to satisfy the claims for additional Shares as nearly as may be in the proportion to the number of Shares already held by them respectively, provided that no Member shall be obliged to take more Shares than he shall have applied for. If any Shares shall not be capable without fractions of being offered to the Members holding that class of Shares in proportion to their existing holdings, the same shall be offered to such Members, or some of them, in such proportions or in such manner as may be determined by lots drawn in regard thereto, and the lots shall be drawn in such manner as the Directors may think fit. Any Shares not taken up in accordance with the foregoing provisions and any Shares released from the provisions of this Article by such Special Resolution as aforesaid shall be under the control of the Directors, who may allot, grant options over or otherwise dispose of the same to such persons, on such terms, and in such manner as they think fit, provided that, in the case of Shares not accepted as aforesaid, such Shares shall not be disposed of on terms which are more favourable to the proposed allottees thereof than the terms on which they were offered to the Members.

(b) Subject to this Article the Directors are unconditionally authorised for the purposes of section 80 of the Act to allot Shares up to the amount of the total unissued Share Capital of the Company (original and increased) for the time being at any time or times during the period of five years from the date of incorporation of the Company or during any further period of renewal of the authority conferred by this Article, whichever is the later.

(c) In accordance with section 91 of the Act, section 89 (1) and section 90 (1) to (6) (inclusive) shall be excluded from applying to the Company.

5. The Company shall be a private company limited by Shares in the sense of section 1 of the Act. No invitation shall be made to the public to subscribe for any Shares or debentures of the Company and the Company and its Directors, officials, agents and all others acting on its behalf are hereby prohibited from making any such invitation to the public.

6. Regulation 5 of Table A shall be amended by adding the words "provided that the Company shall be bound to recognise the trust capacity of persons in respect of whom Shares are entered in the Register of Members of the Company in the names of persons as trustees under a trust to which the Trusts (Scotland) Act 1921 applies and any Deed of Assumption and Conveyance or Minute of Resignation by any such persons shall be recognised by the Company as effecting the purposes therein contained."

Lien

7. The Company shall have a first paramount lien on every Share for (i) all moneys (whether presently payable or not) called or payable at a fixed time in respect of that Share and (ii) for all moneys presently payable by the registered holder thereof or his estate to the Company; but the Directors may at any time declare any Share to be wholly or in part exempt from the provisions of this Article. The Company's lien, if any, on a Share shall extend to all rights attaching thereto and all dividends and sums payable thereon.

Transfer and Transmission of Shares

8. All transfers of Shares must:

(a) be lodged at the Registered Office or such other place as the Directors may appoint and be accompanied by the certificate for the Shares to which it relates and such other evidence as the Directors may reasonably require to show the right of the transferor to make the transfer; and

(b) be in respect of one class of Shares only; and

(c) be in favour of not more than one transferee.

Any direction (by way of renunciation, nomination or otherwise) by a Member entitled to an allotment of Shares to the effect that such Shares or any of them be allotted or issued to or registered in name of some person other than himself shall for the purpose of these Articles be deemed to be a transfer of Shares.

9. The following provisions shall apply to all transfers of Shares:

(a) Any Member proposing to transfer any Shares must give prior written notice to the Company specifying the proposed transferee, the number of Shares proposed to be transferred and in the case of a sale the proposed price per Share, or in the case of any other transfer, the amount which in his opinion constitutes the value per Share. The other Members shall have the right to purchase all (but not only some of) such Shares either at the said proposed price or stated value per Share or the market value per Share fixed by an independent expert as specified in paragraph (c) below.

For the purposes of these Articles the Member proposing to transfer any Shares is called "the Vendor;" the prior written notice he must give is called a "Transfer Notice;" the Shares the Vendor proposes to transfer as specified in a Transfer Notice are called "the Offered Shares," and the other Member or Members purchasing such Shares is/are called "the purchasing Member(s)."

A Transfer Notice authorises the Company to sell all (but not only some of) the Offered Shares to the purchasing

Member(s) as agent of the Vendor, either at the price or value per Share specified in the Transfer Notice or at the market value per Share fixed by the independent expert as specified in paragraph (c) below. Unless all the other Members agree, a Transfer Notice cannot be withdrawn.

(b) The Offered Shares shall be offered to the Members (other than the Vendor) as nearly as may be in proportion to the number of Shares held by them respectively. Such offer shall be made by notice in writing (hereinafter called an "Offer Notice") within seven days after the receipt by the Company of the Transfer Notice.

The Offer Notice shall state the proposed transferee and the price or value per Share specified in the Transfer Notice and shall be open for written acceptance only for a period of 14 days from its date, provided that if a certificate of valuation is requested under paragraph (c) below the offer shall remain open for such written acceptance for a period of 14 days after the date on which notice of the market value certified in accordance with that paragraph is given by the Company to the Members. For the purpose of this Article an offer shall be deemed to be accepted on the day on which the acceptance is received by the Company.

The Offer Notice shall further invite each Member to state in his reply the number of additional Shares (if any) in excess of his proportion which he desires to purchase and if all the Members do not accept the offer in respect of their respective proportions in full the Shares not so accepted shall be used to satisfy the claims for additional Shares as nearly as may be in the proportion to the number of Shares already held by the claimants respectively, provided that no Member shall be obliged to take more Shares than he shall have applied for.

If any Shares shall be capable without fractions of being offered to Members in proportion to their existing holdings, the same shall be offered to the Members, or some of them, in such proportions or in such manner as may be determined by lots drawn in regard thereto, and the lots shall be drawn in such manner as the Directors may think fit.

(c) Any Member may, not later than seven days after the date of the Offer Notice, serve on the Company notice in writing requesting that the market value of the Offered Shares be fixed by an independent Chartered Accountant (who may be the Auditor or Auditors of the Company) mutually chosen by the Vendor and the Member or failing agreement as to such choice nominated on the application of either party by the President for the time being of the Institute of Chartered Accountants of Scotland. Such Accountant (hereinafter called "the Valuer") shall be deemed to act as an expert and not as an arbiter and his determination of the market value shall be final and binding for all purposes hereof. The Valuer shall certify his opinion of the market value of the Offered Shares in writing signed by him. The Valuer's costs shall be borne equally between the Vendor and the Member in question. On receipt of the Valuer's certificate the Company shall by notice in writing inform all Members (including the Vendor) of the market value of the Offered Shares and of the price per Share (being the lower of the price or value specified in the Transfer Notice and the market value of each Share) at which the Offered Shares are offered for sale. For this purpose the market value of each of the Offered Shares shall be the market value of the Offered Shares certified as aforesaid divided by the number of the Offered Shares.

(d) If purchasing Members shall be found for all (but not only some of) the Offered Shares within the relevant period specified in paragraph (b) above, the Company shall not later than seven days after the expiry of such period give notice in writing (hereinafter called a "Sale Notice") to the Vendor specifying the purchasing Members and the Vendor shall be bound upon payment of the price due in respect of all the Offered Shares to transfer the same to the purchasing Members.

(e) If the Vendor shall fail to sign and deliver a valid transfer of any of the Offered Shares which he has become bound to sell pursuant to the foregoing provisions the Secretary of the Company or if the Secretary shall be the Vendor, any Director of the Company other than the Vendor, shall be deemed to have been appointed agent of the Vendor with full power to complete, execute and deliver in the name and on behalf of the Vendor, transfers of the Shares to be sold by him pursuant to these provisions, and to receive payment of the price on his behalf, and to give a valid receipt and discharge therefor. The Directors shall register any transfer granted in pursuance of these powers notwithstanding that the Certificate or Certificates for the Offered Shares may not be produced with such transfer or transfers and after the purchasing Member(s) has/have been registered in exercise of these powers, the validity of the proceedings shall not be questioned by any person.

(f) If no Sale Notice shall be given by the Company to the Vendor within the time limit specified in paragraph (d) above, or if purchasers are not found for all the Offered Shares, the Vendor shall be entitled, for a period of 30 days after the expiry of such time limit, to transfer the Offered Shares to the proposed transferee specified in the Transfer Notice but in the case of a sale, at not less than the lower of the price stated in the Transfer Notice and the market value if this has been fixed by the Valuer, and the Directors shall register such transfer(s).

(g) Any purported transfer of Shares by any Member not preceded by a Transfer Notice given in accordance with the foregoing provisions, shall be of no effect unless the other Members shall have validly waived their rights in writing, and no such purported transfer shall be registered by the Directors.

10. If: (i) any Member who is also a Director shall cease to be a Director for any reason whatever; or

(ii) any Member employed by the Company shall cease to be so employed for any reason whatever or

(iii) any Member shall die or have a curator appointed by any competent court or if he shall become apparently insolvent or if his estate shall be sequestrated or if he shall be declared bankrupt or shall have any receiving order made against him or shall make any arrangement or composition with his creditors generally or shall become of unsound mind or being a Company shall go into liquidation (other than a liquidation for the purpose of reconstruction or amalgamation) or have a receiver appointed over all or any of its assets;

then the following provisions shall apply:

(a) Such Member or the executor, trustee, curator, guardian, liquidator, receiver or other legal representative of such Member (hereinafter collectively and individually referred to in this Article as "the Transferring Shareholder") shall be bound if so required by written notice given by the Directors at any time within six months after the occurrence of the relevant event referred to in paragraphs (i), (ii) or (iii) above, to sell and transfer all (but not only some of) the Shares vested in him to any Member or Members other than the Transferring Shareholder, willing to purchase the same (hereinafter called "the purchasing Member(s)") at such price as the parties may mutually agree or failing such agreement at the market value per Share as at the date of such notice certified in accordance with the provisions of Article 9 (c) hereof.

(b) If the Directors exercise the foregoing power to require a sale, the Shares vested in the Transferring Shareholder shall be offered to the Members other than the Transferring Shareholder in proportion to the number of Shares held by them respectively. Such offer shall be made by notice in writing by the Directors (a copy of which shall at the same time be given to the Transferring Shareholder) proposing a price for the sale and purchase of the Shares. Such offer shall be open for negotiation of such price between the Transferring Shareholder and the other Members (and written acceptance if so agreed) for a period of 14 days from its date. If agreement on the price for the sale and purchase of the Shares is not reached by the expiry of said period of 14 days between the Transferring Shareholder and any other Member(s) wishing to purchase such Shares, any Member shall be entitled by written notice to the Company to require that the market value of the Shares in question be fixed by the Valuer in accordance with the provisions of Article 9 (c) hereof, and on the market value being certified by the Valuer, the Transferring Shareholder shall sell and such other Member(s) shall purchase such Shares at such market value.

The provisions of paragraphs (b), (d) and (e) of Article 9 hereof shall apply *mutatis mutandis* to the sale and transfer of Shares under this Article and the words "Vendor" and "Offered Shares" where they appear in those paragraphs of Article 9 shall for the purposes of this Article mean the Transferring Shareholder and the Shares vested in the Transferring Shareholder respectively.

(c) The Members who purchase the Shares of any other Member pursuant to the foregoing provisions shall procure that any personal guarantee or security granted by such Member for the indebtedness of the Company is released or discharged on the date of completion of such purchase.

11. To the end of Regulation 29 of Table A there shall be added "provided that nothing in this Regulation shall apply to Shares held by two or more persons as trustees under a trust to which the Trusts (Scotland) Act 1921 applies."

General Meetings

12. There shall be added at the end of Regulation 41 of Table A the words "and at such adjourned meeting the Members or Member present personally or by proxy shall be a quorum and shall be entitled to proceed with the business of the Meeting and exercise thereat all powers of the Members in General Meeting to the intent that no Member or Members shall have the power by absence from Meetings to frustrate the business of the Company."

13. In paragraph (b) of Regulation 46 of Table A the words "one or more" shall be substituted for the words "at least two." Paragraphs (c) and (d) of said Regulation 46 shall be omitted.

14. On a poll votes may be given either personally or by proxy. A Member may appoint only one proxy in respect of his entire holding of each class of Shares in the Company.

Directors

15. Unless otherwise determined by Ordinary Resolution the number of Directors (other than Alternate Directors) shall not be subject to any maximum and there may be a sole Director. A sole Director shall have authority to exercise all the powers and discretions by Table A or these Articles expressed to be vested in the Directors generally and Regulations 89 and 90 of Table A shall be modified accordingly.

Borrowing Powers

16. The Directors, without prejudice to their general powers, may in the name and on behalf of the Company and from time to time at their discretion borrow from themselves or from others any sum or sums of money for the purposes of the Company without limit as to amount and mortgage or charge the undertaking, property and uncalled Capital of the Company or any part thereof as security for any debt, liability or obligation of the Company or of any third party and that upon such terms and in such manner as they think fit.

Proceedings of Directors

17. The Directors may appoint a person who is willing to act to be a Director either to fill a vacancy or as an additional Director provided that the appointment does not cause the number of Directors to exceed any number fixed by or in accordance with these Articles as the maximum number of Directors.

18. The Directors shall not be liable to retirement by rotation and Regulations 78 and 84 of Table A shall be varied accordingly.

19. There shall be added to the end of Regulation 87 of Table A the following:

"The Directors may similarly provide such benefits and make such contributions and payments for any person who is a Director of and who has held but no longer holds any executive office or employment with any other company the directors of which the Company is authorised by its Memorandum of Association to benefit notwithstanding that he may be or have been a Director of the Company."

20. A Director may vote as a Director in regard to any contract or arrangement in which he is interested or upon any matter arising

therefrom, and if he shall so vote shall be counted and he shall be reckoned in estimating a quorum when any such contract or arrangement is under consideration.

21. Any one or more of the Directors or any Committee of the Directors may participate in a meeting of the Directors or of such Committee (a) by means of a conference telephone or similar communications equipment allowing all persons participating in the meeting to hear each other at the same time or (b) by a succession of telephone calls or similar communications to Directors from the Chairman of the meeting following disclosure to them of all material points. Participating by such means shall constitute presence in person at a meeting. Such meeting shall be deemed to have occurred in (a) at the place where most of the Directors participating are present and in (b) at the place where the Chairman of the meeting is present.

Names and Addresses of Subscribers

Dated at this day of Nineteen hundred and ninety

Witness to the above signatures:

Note: Following upon the Companies (Single Member Private Limited Companies) Regulations 1992 a private limited company can be incorporated with only one subscriber to the Memorandum of Association

Schedule 9

DEADLOCK PROVISIONS

(a) If a deadlock in management of the Company arises, any Member shall be entitled to convene an Extraordinary General Meeting of the Company, to consider and if possible, settle the subject matter of such deadlock. If such Meeting fails to resolve such deadlock, then any Member shall be entitled to convene a further Extraordinary General Meeting of the Company by notice given not earlier than 14 days and not later than 30 days after the date of said first Meeting, to further consider the subject matter of such deadlock with a view to resolving same. If no such second Meeting is so convened, or if the subject matter of such deadlock is not resolved at such second Meeting, then Notice to Terminate (as defined in paragraph (c) of this Clause) may thereafter be given, but not earlier than 14 days after the date of said second Meeting if such second Meeting is so convened or 14 days after the date of said first Meeting if no such second Meeting is convened, and not later than the expiry of 30 days after said first or second mentioned meeting as the case may be.

(b) If Notice to Terminate is given the holder(s) of a majority in nominal value of the issued Shares of the class which did not give the Notice to Terminate shall have the option for a period of 14 days from service of the Notice to Terminate to acquire all (but not only some of) the issued Shares of the other class at the market value thereof as at the date of exercise of such option, determined by an independent expert appointed in terms of Article [9(c)] hereof. Such option shall be exercised by the holder(s) of a majority in nominal value of the issued Shares of the class which did not give the Notice to Terminate, giving written notice of exercise of such option to the Secretary of the Company (who shall on receipt communicate same to all the Shareholders other than those giving such notice) within such period of 14 days from service of the Notice to Terminate. Upon determination of the market value of the said Shares by the independent expert, he shall advise all Shareholders of such market value and not later than seven days thereafter, the holders of all the issued Shares of the class which gave the Notice to Terminate (and not only the majority who gave such Notice) shall deliver valid transfers of all their Shares with the relevant Certificate(s) therefor, in exchange for payment of the relevant price. If, after Notice to Terminate is given, the holders of a majority in nominal value of the issued Shares of the class which did not give such Notice do not exercise such option within the said period of 14 days, then the holders of a majority in nominal value of the issued Shares of the class which did give the Notice to Terminate shall have the option for a period of 14 days from the expiry of the said first period of 14 days to acquire all (but only some of) the issued Shares of the other class, at the market value thereof, on the same terms and conditions *mutatis mutandis* as above specified.

(c) For the purpose of these provisions, Notice to Terminate means written notice given by the holder(s) of a majority in nominal value of the issued A or B Shares as the case may be. Notice to Terminate shall be given to the Secretary of the Company (who shall on receipt communicate same to all the Shareholders other than those giving such Notice).

(d) Shares to be acquired pursuant to the provisions of this Article following the exercise of the relevant option before specified by the holder(s) of a majority of the issued Shares of one class shall be offered at the market value thereof to all the holders of issued Shares of that class, in proportion to the number of Shares held by them respectively in accordance *mutatis mutandis* with the provisions of Article [9(b)] hereof, and not only to the majority who made such offer.

(e) The Members who purchase the Shares of any other Member pursuant to the foregoing provisions shall procure that any personal guarantee or security granted by such Member for the indebtedness of the Company is released or discharged on the date of completion of such purchase.

Schedule 10

STATUTORY REGISTERS

REGISTER OF MEMBERS — Page No.:

Company :

Class of Share :

Name :

Address :

Date	Transfer or Allotment and Serial No. thereof	*Shares Acquired*		*Shares disposed of*		Balance of Holding
		Price paid or Subscribed	No. of Shares acquired	Price paid	No. of Shares disposed of	

REGISTER OF DIRECTORS

Name of Company:

Date Appointed	:	Date Resigned	:
Name of Director	:	Nationality	:
Former Name (if any)	:		
Address	:	Occupation	:
		Date of Birth	:

Other Directorships:

REGISTER OF SECRETARIES

Company:

Name and any former Name	Address	Date of Appointment/ Resignation

REGISTER OF DIRECTORS' INTERESTS IN SHARES OR DEBENTURES

Company:

Class of Share
or Debenture:

Director	No. of Shares or Debentures	Name in which registered and nature of interest	Date and event notified	Consideration

REGISTER OF CHARGES

Company:

Date of Charge : Date of Registration :

Type of Charge :

Amount Secured :

Particulars of
Property charged :

Name(s) and Address(es)
of Creditor(s) :

Amount of Commission paid :

REGISTER OF ALLOTMENTS

Company

Class of Shares:

No.	Name and Address	No. of Shares applied for and allotted	Amount Payable	Date of Payment

REGISTER OF TRANSFERS

Company:

Class of Shares:

Date	No. of Transfer	No. of Shares Transferred	Value	Transferor Name	Transferee Name

Schedule 11

PAPERS FOR TAKING A POLL

* RESOLUTION NO.				
		Votes Cast		
Name of Shareholder	No. of voting shares held	For the Resolution	Against the Resolution	Remarks

[*] LIMITED
(Company No.)

STATEMENT RECORDING VOTES ON A POLL

In respect of the Resolutions considered at the Annual General Meeting of the Members of the Company held at [*] on [*] at [*] and voted on by those Members.

* RESOLUTION NO.				
		Votes Cast		
Name of Shareholder	No. of voting shares held	For the Resolution	Against the Resolution	Remarks

The Chairman
[*] Limited,

We, the scrutineers appointed at the Annual General Meeting of the members of the Company held at [*] on [*] at [*] noon to take the/poll on the Resolutions considered at the meeting and voted on by those members hereby report that the result of the poll was as follows:

Resolution No.	Votes Cast for the Resolution*			Votes Cast against the Resolution*			Majority	
	In Person	By Proxy	Total	In Person	By Proxy	Total	For Resolution	Against Resolution
Resolution 1								
Resolution 2								
Resolution 3								
Resolution 4								
Resolution 5								

....

....

....

....

*Leave blank those Resolutions where no poll taken

SCHEDULE 12

SERVICE CONTRACT

THIS AGREEMENT is made the day of 19

BETWEEN:-

(1) LIMITED, (No. ....) having its Registered Office at

(hereinafter called "the Company") ....of the first part;

(2) residing at (hereinafter called "the Executive")

.......................of the second part;

WHEREAS

1. The company carries on business as [...].

2. The Executive is [is to be] employed as [...] of the Company on the terms and conditions hereinafter set forth.

NOW THEREFORE the parties hereby CONTRACT and AGREE as follows:

1. *Definitions*:

In this Contract unless the context otherwise requires the following expressions shall have the following meanings:

"Associated Company" any company which for the time being is the holding company (as defined by section 736 of the Companies Act 1985) of the Company and any subsidiary of such holding company, any company of which the equity share capital (as defined in section 744 of the Companies Act 1985) is owned as to 50 per cent or less but more than 25 per cent by such holding company or by any of its subsidiaries, or by the Company or any of its subsidiaries as the case may be, and including a subsidiary of an Associated Company.

"the Board"	the Directors of the Company present at a meeting of the Directors or of a Committee of the Directors duly convened and held.
"the Commencement Date"	the day of 199 , notwithstanding the date(s) hereof.
"the Group"	the Company and its Subsidiaries and Associated Companies from time to time.
"Group Company"	any Subsidiary or Associated Company of the Group.
"Subsidiary"	any Company which for the time being is a subsidiary (as defined by section 736 of the Companies Act 1985) of the Company.
"the Appointment"	the employment of the Executive by the Company under the terms of this Contract.

2. *Appointment*

2.1. The Company shall employ the Executive and the Executive shall serve the Company as full time [......................] for the period specified in Clause 3.

2.2 The Company may at any time require the Executive to serve any other Group Company or Companies and to carry out for such Group Company or Companies such duties and responsibilities as may be assigned by the Board, but otherwise on the same terms and conditions as to salary and otherwise as herein provided.

3. *Duration*

3.1 The Appointment shall continue for an initial period of three years from the Commencement Date, subject [to the provisions of Clause [Review of Performance] and] to the provisions for termination in Clause 14.

3.2 Either party shall have the right to terminate the Appointment on the third anniversary of the Commencement Date, by giving the other not less than [six] months' prior written notice of termination.

3.3 If not so terminated on the third anniversary of the Commencement Date, the Appointment shall thereafter continue for successive periods of three years, unless and until terminated on the expiry of any such period of three years by either party giving the other not less than [six] months' prior written notice of termination.

OR

3.1 The Appointment shall continue for an initial period of [............] years from the Commencement Date.

3.2 Either party shall have the right to terminate the Appointment on the expiry of said initial period by giving the other not less than [............] months' prior written notice of termination.

3.3 If not so terminated at the end of said initial period the Appointment shall thereafter continue from year to year unless and until terminated by either party giving the other not less than [............] months' prior written notice of termination to expire on any anniversary of the Commencement Date.

4. *Duties of Executive*

4.1 The Executive shall act as full time [............] of the Company, in accordance with the directions of the Board from time to time, and shall perform such specific functions as the Board may from time to time delegate to him/her.

4.2 The Executive's usual hours of work shall be [9.00 am to 5.30 pm] on business days, plus such additional time as may reasonably be required from time to time for the proper fulfilment of his/her duties and responsibilities hereunder. For the avoidance of doubt, no overtime or other additional remuneration shall be payable for any such additional time worked.

OR

4.1 The Executive shall undertake such duties and responsibilities in relation to the Company or any Group Company as the Board may from time to time delegate to him/her at such place or places in the United Kingdom or elsewhere as the Company shall reasonably specify, and shall carry out all lawful and reasonable resolutions of the Board from time to time.

4.2 The Executive shall promote the trade and business of the Company and the Group to the best of his/her ability, knowledge and power and shall not willingly or knowingly do or permit to be done anything to the prejudice of the Company or the Group or any trade or business carried on by the Company or any Group Company.

4.3 The Executive's usual hours of work shall be [9.00 am to 5.30 pm] on business days, plus such additional time as may reasonably be required from time to time for the proper fulfilment of his/her duties and responsibilities hereunder. For the avoidance of doubt, no overtime or other additional remuneration shall be payable for any such additional time worked.

[*Review of Performance*

4.4 The Board shall review the Executive's performance in carrying out the Appointment, not earlier than [six] and not more than [nine] months after the Commencement Date.

4.5 In light of the Board's assessment of the Executive's performance, the Company shall have the right, in its unfettered discretion, to terminate the Appointment, by giving not less than [three] months' notice of termination before the expiry of such [nine] months after the Commencement Date.

4.6 If following such review, notice of termination is not so given, such right of termination on the part of the Company shall lapse, and the Appointment may thereafter be terminated only in accordance with Clauses [3 and 14.]

4.7 Notwithstanding the foregoing the Company shall be under no obligation, for a period of [12] months, or at any time after notice of termination of the Appointment shall have been given by either party, to vest in or assign to the Executive any powers or duties or to provide any work for the Executive, and the Company may at any time suspend the Executive from the performance of his duties or exclude him from any premises of the Company and need not give any reason for so-doing, but his salary will not cease to be payable by reason only of such suspension or exclusion of the Executive (unless and until his employment under this Agreement shall be determined under any provision hereof).

5 *Remuneration*

5.1 As remuneration for his/her services hereunder, the Executive shall be paid a fixed salary of THOUSAND POUNDS (£) per annum, payable monthly in arrear. Such fixed salary shall be deemed to accrue from day to day, and shall be [inclusive] [exclusive] of any fees payable to the Executive as a Director of the Company and/or any Group Company.

5.2 Such fixed salary shall be subject to annual review by the Company, and may be increased (but not decreased) by such amount as the Board in its discretion may think fit.

5.3 In addition to the fixed salary above specified, the Executive shall be entitled to an annual bonus [of such amount as the

Board in its sole discretion may determine] of an amount equal to [............] per cent of the net profit before tax of the Company [of the Group] as certified by the Auditors for the time being of the Company [Group].

5.4 Such bonus shall be paid to the Executive not later than [seven] days after the Accounts of the Company [Group] have been certified by the Auditors [and in any event not later than [ten] months after the end of the financial year in question of the Company [Group].

5.5 Such bonus shall not be deemed to accrue until the end of the financial year by reference to which it is to be calculated, and if the Appointment is terminated for any reason whatever before the end of such financial year, no part of such bonus shall be payable to the Executive.

OR

5.5 If the Appointment is terminated for any reason before the end of the financial year by reference to which such bonus is calculated, the Executive shall be entitled to a proportionate part of such bonus, calculated on a time basis as if the amount of such bonus which would have been payable if the Appointment had continued to the end of such financial year accrued at a uniform daily rate.

6. *Pension, etc.*

[6.1 With effect from [the Commencement Date] the Executive shall be entitled to join the Company's Pension Scheme [specify life assurance or health scheme if appropriate] [on a non-contributory basis].] [The Company may require the Executive to contribute to the Pension Scheme provided that such contributions do not exceed 5 per cent of the Executive's salary (excluding bonus) from time to time.]

[6.1 With effect from [the Commencement Date] [the Company shall pay an amount equal to [............] per cent of the Executive's salary from time to time (at the rate then payable under Clause 5 hereof) by way of contributions to an existing approved pension scheme, such amounts to be paid in addition to the remuneration set out in Clause 5 and to be payable monthly].

6.2 The Executive shall be entitled to participate at the Company's expense in the Company's permanent health insurance scheme and [for himself, his spouse and dependent children (if any)] in the Company's private medical expenses insurance scheme [corporate band [............]], subject always to the rules of the schemes [details of which are available from the personnel department.]

6.3 The Executive shall submit to such medical examinations as may be reasonably required by the Board and/or the insurers under the policy referred to in Clause 6.2 from time to time, such medical examinations to be carried out by a registered medical practitioner nominated by the Board. The Executive hereby irrevocably authorises and gives his consent, for the purposes of Section 3 of the Access to Medical Reports Act 1988, to such medical practitioner to disclose to the Board and/or the insurers under the policy referred to in Clause 6.2 the results of such examinations and such other relevant medical information as the Board may reasonably require and to discuss any matter arising from such examinations with an authorised representative of the Board. Copies of any reports made and information provided to the Board and/or such insurers in terms of this Clause 6.3 shall be made available to the Executive. The fees and expenses incurred in the provision of such medical examinations and obtaining of such medical information shall be borne by the Company.

6.4 If in the opinion of the [Board] [Remuneration Committee] [(acting reasonably)] the cost to the Company of maintaining (in respect of the Executive [or, in the case of the private medical expenses insurance scheme, the Executive, his spouse and his dependent children (if any)]) the permanent health insurance scheme and/or the private medical expenses insurance scheme becomes unreasonably expensive, the Company [acting through the Remuneration Committee] shall be entitled to reduce the level of the benefit provided under the permanent health insurance scheme or private medical expenses insurance scheme (as the case may be) provided that the cost to the Company is not less than the cost in relation to the permanent health insurance scheme or private medical expenses insurance scheme (as the case may be) in force at that date (or as soon as practicable thereafter) [increased in line with the total increases in the Index from that date]. The Company shall give the Executive reasonable notice of its decision to reduce the benefits provided under the permanent health insurance scheme and/or the private medical expenses insurance scheme pursuant to this Clause.

6.5 If it is not possible for the Executive to participate in the Company's permanent health insurance scheme or for the Executive, his spouse and dependent children (if any) to participate in the Company's private medical expenses insurance scheme due to the Executive or family member, pursuant to the medical examinations referred to in Clause 6.3, or for any other reason being declared uninsurable by the insurers then the Company shall be under no obligation to provide such insurance benefits to the Executive and for the avoidance of doubt shall not be deemed for this reason to be in breach of this Clause 6.

7. *Motor Car*

7.1 Throughout the duration of the Appointment, the Company shall provide the Executive with a suitable motor car, which shall be replaced not less frequently than [every two years].

7.2 The Company shall pay the taxation, insurance premiums and running expenses of such motor car including petrol [but not petrol for private use], maintenance and repairs.

7.3 The Executive shall be entitled to make use of such motor car for his/her own private purposes.

7.4 The Executive shall at all times conform with all rules and regulations which the Company may from time to time impose in respect of motor cars provided by the Company for the use of its employees.

8. *Expenses*

The Company shall reimburse the Executive the full amount of all travel, accommodation and other expenses properly incurred by the Executive on the business of the Company and the Group, subject to production of such receipts or other vouchers as the Company may reasonably require.

9. *Holidays*

9.1 In addition to public holidays, the Executive shall be entitled to [............] working days paid holiday in each holiday year to be taken at such times as may be agreed with the Board.

9.2 Such holiday entitlement shall accrue uniformly at the rate of one-twelfth of such annual entitlement per complete month worked after the Commencement Date, but unless otherwise agreed by the Company, holiday entitlement accrued but not taken by the end of each holiday year may not be carried forward, nor shall the Executive be entitled to payment in lieu.

9.3 For the purpose of calculating holiday entitlement hereunder, the Company and Group's "holiday year" runs from [lst January] to [31st December].

10. *Illness, etc.*

10.1 If the Executive is prevented by illness or injury from performing his/her duties and responsibilities hereunder, he/she shall [if so requested by the Board furnish the Board with medical evidence reasonably satisfactory to the Board] or [notify the Company on the first day of such illness or injury and provide the Company with a completed self certificate form by the fourth day of such illness or injury. If such illness or injury lasts longer than seven days, a Doctor's Certificate must be provided to the Company by the eighth day].

10.2 In the event of such illness or injury, the Executive shall (subject to providing the appropriate certificate(s) as specified above) be entitled to the following payments:

(i) During any continuous period of [ninety] days or the first [ninety] days in aggregate in any period of twelve consecutive calendar months—the full amount of his/her fixed salary (but not bonus); and

(ii) During any further period of [ninety] days or the next [ninety] days in aggregate in any period of twelve consecutive calendar months—50 per cent of such fixed salary (but not bonus).

10.3 If such illness or injury continues beyond any continuous period in excess of [one hundred and eighty] days or [one hundred and eighty] days in aggregate in any period of twelve consecutive calendar months, any further payment beyond that specified in sub-paragraph 10.2 (ii) above shall be at the company's sole discretion.

10.4 The above provisions do not affect the Company's right of termination under Clause 14.

11. *Outside Appointments*

Throughout the duration of the Appointment the Executive shall not without the prior written consent of the Company accept or hold any appointment or office with any company, firm or business outwith the Group, or with any public body, board, local authority or Government Department.

12. *Inventions*

12.1 Subject to the Executive's statutory rights under the Patents Act 1977, the Copyright, Designs and Patents Act 1988 and any other applicable Act, any invention, discovery, process, design, plan, computer program or other intellectual property whatever, and any modification enhancement or development of any existing such thing (hereinafter referred to as "Inventions") made or discovered by the Executive (whether alone or with others) while in the employment of the Company or the Group in connection with or in any way affecting or relating to the business of the Company or the Group or capable of being used or adapted for use therein shall forthwith be disclosed to the Company and shall belong to and be the absolute property of the Company or such Group Company as the Company may nominate for this purpose.

12.2 If so required by the Company (whether before or after the termination of the Appointment) the Executive shall at the Company's expense, apply or join in applying for letters patent registration or other appropriate protection in the United Kingdom or elsewhere in the world, for any Inventions, and execute all documents and do all other things necessary, expedient or desirable to vest such letters patent registered rights or other protection when obtained, and all right, title and interest in and to the same, in the Company or such Group Company as sole beneficial owner, and for this purpose shall, at the Company's expense, take or defend any proceedings to procure or defend such application registration or protection.

12.3 The Executive hereby irrevocably appoints the Company to be his/her attorney in his/her name and on his/her behalf to execute any such document or do any such thing, and generally to use the Executive's name for the purpose of giving to the Company or any such Group Company the full benefit of the provisions of this Clause.

13. *Confidentiality*

Save as specifically authorised by the Company, or as required in the performance of his/her duties hereunder, the Executive shall at all times (both during and after the termination of the Appointment) maintain absolute confidentiality in respect of all trade secrets, secret or confidential operations, know-how processes or dealings, inventions, discoveries, processes, designs, plans, computer programs and other intellectual property whatever and all information concerning the organisation, business, finances, transactions and affairs, of the Company and the Group which have come or may come to his/her knowledge during the Appointment, and shall not disclose any of same (and if disclosure is authorised by the Company, shall make disclosure only under the terms of the Company's current Confidentiality Agreement) to any other person, firm, company, body or authority, or use or attempt to use any such information in any manner which may injure or cause loss or may be calculated to injure or cause loss directly or indirectly to the Company or the Group.

14. *Termination*

14.1 The Appointment may be terminated at any time by the Company giving written notice of immediate termination to the Executive in any of the following events:

(i) If the Executive is prevented by illness or injury from performing his/her duties hereunder for a continuous period in excess of [one hundred and eighty days] or for more than an aggregate of [one hundred and eighty days] in any period of twelve consecutive calendar months; or

(ii) If the Executive is guilty of any act of serious misconduct or wilful neglect or other conduct calculated or likely prejudicially to affect the interests of the Company or the Group; or

(iii) If the Executive commits any material breach of the terms of this Contract which cannot be remedied or, if it can be remedied, remains unremedied on the expiry of [seven] days after the Executive has received written notice from the Company specifying the breach and the action required to remedy the same; or

(iv) If the Executive becomes bankrupt or is sequestrated or makes any arrangement or composition with his/ her creditors generally; or

(v) Becomes of unsound mind or becomes a patient within the meaning of the [Mental Health (Scotland) Act 1986] [Mental Health Act 1983]; or

(vi) Is convicted of any criminal offence, whether committed during or outwith normal business hours, other than a motoring or other offence which in the reasonable opinion of the Board does not affect the Executive's position under the Appointment; or

(vii) Is disqualified from holding office as a Director pursuant to an order under the Company Directors Disqualification Act 1986;

(viii) If the Executive is, in the reasonable opinion of the Board, incompetent in the performance of his duties; or

(ix) If the Executive commits any act of dishonesty whether relating to the Company, any of its employees or otherwise.

14.2 On termination of the Appointment for any reason whatever, the Executive shall:

(i) Deliver up to the Company all books, documents, papers, data (in whatever medium the same be stored or recorded) and other materials and property relating to the business of the Company or the Group which may then be in his/ her possession or under his/her control; and

(ii) On request of the Company resign (waiving all claims for compensation of any nature in respect thereof) from office as a Director of the Company and/or any Group Company of which he/she is then a Director (but such resignation shall be without prejudice to any claim to which the Executive may be entitled under the Employment Rights Act 1996) and in the event of failing to do so, the Company shall be entitled (and is hereby irrevocably authorised by the Executive) in name and on behalf of the Executive to execute any documents and do any other thing necessary to effect such resignation and the intimation or registration thereof.

14.3 This Agreement shall automatically terminate on the Executive reaching his [65th] birthday.

14.4 In order to investigate a complaint against the Executive of misconduct the Company is entitled to suspend the Executive on full pay for so long as may be necessary to carry out a proper investigation and hold a disciplinary hearing.

15. *Non-Competition*

15.1 Throughout the duration of the Appointment, the Executive shall not, unless otherwise agreed in writing by the Company, directly or indirectly carry on or be engaged or concerned or interested (whether as partner, consultant, employee, shareholder, director, sub-contractor, agent or otherwise) in any other trade or business PROVIDED THAT this provision shall not prohibit the Executive from holding or being otherwise interested in not more than [three] per cent of the equity share capital or loan capital of any company which is quoted on a recognised investment exchange (as defined in the Financial Services Act 1986).

15.2 The Executive shall not for a period of [one year] from the date of termination of the Appointment directly or indirectly carry on or be engaged or concerned or interested (whether as partner, consultant, employee, shareholder, director, sub-contractor, agent or otherwise), in any trade or business carried on within a radius of [ ] miles of any premises from which the Company carries on business which is or is in any way calculated or likely to be competitive with or similar to any trade or business carried on by the Company at any time during the period of twelve months preceding such date of termination; And the provisions of this sub-paragraph shall apply also to any trade or business of any Group Company which the Executive has served during the Appointment.

15.3 The Executive shall not for a period of [one year] from the termination of the Appointment directly or indirectly by any means whatsoever, and whether for himself/herself or for or on behalf of any third party, canvass or solicit orders or instructions for goods or services of the same kind or nature as, or competitive or calculated or likely to be competitive with, those with which the Company (or any Group Company which the Executive has served during the Appointment) was concerned to a material extent at any time during the twelve months preceding such date of termination, from any person, firm, company, body or authority who or which was a customer, supplier, agent or distributor of the Company (or any Group Company which the Executive has served during the Appointment) or with whom or which the Company (or any Group Company which the Executive has served during the Appointment) has otherwise done business during such period of twelve months.

15.4 The Executive shall not for a period of [one year] from the date of termination of the Appointment induce or endeavour to induce any person with whom the Company (or any Group Company which the Executive has served during the

Appointment) has done business at any time within twelve months prior to the date of such termination, to remove their business from the Company (or any such Group Company).

15.5 The Executive shall not for a period of [one year] from the date of termination of the Appointment directly or indirectly by any means whatsoever, and whether for himself/herself or for or on behalf of any third party, solicit, endeavour to entice away, offer employment to, employ or cause to be employed any person who at any time during the twelve months prior to such termination is or was a senior employee of the Company (or any Group Company which the executive has served during the Appointment).

15.6 If any of the foregoing undertakings is held for any reason not to be valid or enforceable as going beyond what is reasonable for the protection of the interests of the Company or the Group, but would be valid if part of the wording were deleted or its extent reduced or modified, then such undertakings shall apply with such modifications or variations as may be necessary to make them enforceable, and any such modification or variation shall not thereby affect the validity of any of the other undertakings.

15.7 The Executive acknowledges and agrees that he/she has taken independent professional advice in relation to the provisions of this Clause, and that such provisions are fair and reasonable.

16. *Other Agreements*

This contract sets out the whole terms and conditions applicable to the Appointment and the Executive's employment by the Company. All prior contracts and agreements (whether reduced to writing or not) in relation to the Executive's employment by the Company or any Group Company are hereby entirely superseded.

17. *Statutory Intimation*

For the purposes of the Employment Rights Act 1996, the terms of employment applying as at the Commencement Date are as specified in the Schedule annexed.

18. *Notices*

18.1 Any notice or other document required or permitted to be given or served under this Contract, may be given or served personally or by leaving the same or sending the same by first class Recorded Delivery post at or to the registered office of the Company, or the address of the Executive as stated in this Contract, or such other address as the Executive may hereafter intimate in writing to the Company for the giving of notice.

18.2 Any such notice or document shall be deemed to have been served:

(i) if delivered, at the time of delivery, or

(ii) if posted, at the expiry of 48 hours after posting.

In proving such service it shall be sufficient to prove that delivery was made or that the envelope containing such notice or document was properly addressed and posted as a pre-paid class Recorded Delivery Letter.

19. *General*

19.1 Any reference to any provision of any Act of Parliament or subordinate legislation pursuant thereto shall be deemed to be a reference to such Act of Parliament or subordinate legislation as amended, modified or re-enacted (whether before or after the date hereof) and any references to any provision of any such Act or legislation shall also include any provision of which they are re-enactments and any provision in repealed enactments.

19.2 Clause headings have been inserted for convenience only and shall not affect the construction of this Contract.

19.3 Notwithstanding termination of this Contract for any reason whatever, the provisions of Clauses 12 (Inventions), 13 (Confidentiality) and 15 (Non-Competition) shall remain in force indefinitely or for the periods therein specified as the case may be.

20. *Applicable Law*

This Contract shall be governed by and construed according to the law of [England and Wales] [Scotland]: IN WITNESS WHEREOF these presents consisting of this and the preceding pages are executed by the parties in duplicate on the date first above mentioned as follows:

Executed for and on behalf of the
said LIMITED by:

....
Director/Secretary

Subscribed by the said
before the undernoted witness:

Witness: ....
Name: ....
Address: ....
.... The Executive
Occupation: ....

SCHEDULE

(i) Job title:

(ii) Date of Commencement: The Commencement Date. No previous employment [The Executive's previous employment with [............] from 19......] shall count with the Appointment as a continuous period of employment.

(iii) Place of Work:

(iv) Hours: See Clause 4.

(v) Remuneration: See Clause 5.

(vi) Holidays: See Clause 9.

(vii) Sickness or Injury: See Clause 10. The Company operates the Statutory Self-Certification and Sick Pay Schemes.

(viii) Pension: The Director is entitled to membership of the Company's Pension Scheme (see Clause 6). A contracting out certificate is in force in respect of the Appointment. [or] [A contracting out certificate is not in force in respect of the Appointment.]

(ix) Notice: See Clauses 2 and 14.

(x) Grievance Procedure: The Executive shall refer any grievance about the Appointment or any dissatisfaction with any disciplinary decision relating to him/her to the Board in writing. The Board will consider the matter and its decision shall be final.

[or]

[All disciplinary decisions concerning the Executive shall be made by the Board. The Board shall consider the Executive's conduct at a duly convened meeting at which the Executive shall be entitled to be present, making such submissions and producing such documents and evidence in support or explanation of his/her conduct as he/she may think fit. All disciplinary decisions made by the Board shall be implemented in such manner as the Board may decide. The Executive shall have no right of appeal from any disciplinary decision made by the Board. The Company reserves the right to suspend the Executive on full pay for any period if, by reason of a requirement to investigate the Director's conduct or for any other reasonable cause, the Company considers it is in the best interests of the Company to do so.]

(xi) The term of the Appointment and the date of termination: see Clause 3.

(xii) Collective Agreements affecting the Appointment are as follows:

(xiii) The Executive may, should his duties so require from time to time be obliged to work outside the United Kingdom ("UK") for periods of in excess of one month. However, (save with the consent of the Executive) no single period of work outside the

UK shall exceed [............ months] and no successive periods of work outside the UK shall exceed a total of [............] months in any single twelve month period.

The Executive shall not be required to reside on a permanent basis outside the UK without his consent. Whilst working outside the UK the Executive's salary may continue to be paid wholly in £ Sterling or may be paid partly in £ Sterling and partly in such local currency as the Company considers appropriate [provided that (save with the Executive's consent) no more than [............ per cent] of the Executive's salary must be paid in a currency other than £ Sterling].

The Executive shall not, other than the reimbursement of expenses incurred in the performance of his duties, be entitled to any extra remuneration or allowance in respect of overseas employment].

.... Director/Secretary
.... Executive

Schedule 13

APPLICATION FOR ADMISSION AS MEMBER OF GUARANTEE COMPANY

APPLICATION FOR ADMISSION AS A MEMBER OF LIMITED, A COMPANY LIMITED BY GUARANTEE AND NOT HAVING A SHARE CAPITAL.

I, (insert full name in capitals) apply to become a member of the Company on the terms and subject to the conditions set out in the Memorandum and Articles of Association of the Company and I understand that every such member undertakes to contribute to the assets of the Company in the event of the same being wound up during the time that he/she is a member or within one year after he/she ceases to be a member for payment of the debts and liabilities of the Company contracted before he/she ceased to be a member and of the costs, charges and expenses of winding up and for the adjustment of the rights of contributories among themselves, such amount as may be required not exceeding [£5.00].

Signature .... Date ....

NAME ....

ADDRESS ....

....

....

....

....

SCHEDULE 14

CHANGE OF NAME

LIMITED

Notice to Members requisitioning Extraordinary General Meeting

Notice is hereby given that an Extraordinary General Meeting of the above named Company will be held at on the day of Nineteen hundred and for the purpose of considering and if thought fit passing the following resolution as a SPECIAL RESOLUTION:

THAT the name of the Company be changed to

Dated at this day of Nineteen hundred and .
By order of the Board.

Secretaries.
Note: A Member entitled to attend and vote may appoint a proxy to attend and, on a poll, to vote in his stead. A proxy need not be a Member of the Company.

Consent to Short Notice

We, the undersigned, being a majority of the Members of the above named Company having a right to attend and vote at the above meeting being a majority together holding not less than Ninety five per cent in nominal value of the shares giving a right to attend and vote at the said Meeting hereby consent to the convening of the said Extraordinary General Meeting at the day and place above mentioned for the passing of the Special Resolution above set forth.

LIMITED
(COMPANY NO.)

MINUTE OF EXTRAORDINARY GENERAL MEETING
of the above named Company
held at the Registered Office on

Present	:	
Notice	:	The Notice calling the Meeting including Minute of Consent to short notice was duly read.
Quorum	:	The Chairman declared a quorum present and the Meeting duly convened.
Change of Name	:	It was resolved by Special Resolution that the name of the Company be changed to [ ]
Closure of Meeting	:	The business of the Meeting having been concluded the Chairman declared the Meeting closed.

____

Chairman

The Companies Acts 1985 and 1989

Private Company Limited by Shares

SPECIAL RESOLUTION OF [ ] LIMITED
(COMPANY NO.)

At an Extraordinary General Meeting of the Members of the above named Company duly convened and held at on the day of Nineteen hundred and the following Resolution was passed as a SPECIAL RESOLUTION:

THAT the name of the Company be changed to

Certified a true copy

____

Company Secretaries

The Companies Acts 1985 and 1989

Company Limited by Shares

WRITTEN RESOLUTION OF LIMITED

(COMPANY NO.)

WE, of and of being the holders of the whole issued Share Capital of the above named Company hereby resolve that the resolution set out hereafter be and is hereby passed as a Special Resolution of the Company, videlicet:

SPECIAL RESOLUTION

That the name of the Company be and is hereby changed to

Dated this day of 19

....

....

SCHEDULE 15

DORMANT COMPANY

LIMITED

Notice to Members requesting Annual General Meeting

Notice is hereby given that the Annual General Meeting of the above named Company will be held at on the day of Nineteen hundred and for the purpose of transacting the ordinary business of the Company and considering and if thought fit passing the following resolution as a SPECIAL RESOLUTION:

THAT the Company, being a dormant company in terms of section 250 of the Companies Act 1985, dispense with the appointment of Auditors.

Dated at this day of Nineteen hundred and
By order of the Board

Company Secretaries.

Note: A Member entitled to attend and vote may appoint a proxy to attend and, on a poll, to vote in his stead. A proxy need not be a Member of the Company.

We, the undersigned, being all of the Members of the above named Company having a right to attend and vote at the above meeting hereby consent to the convening of the said Annual General Meeting at the day and place above mentioned for the passing of the Special Resolution above set forth and for the consideration of the ordinary business of the Company.

LIMITED

MINUTE OF ANNUAL GENERAL MEETING of the above named Company held at

the Registered Office on

PRESENT	:	
NOTICE	:	The Notice calling the Meeting including Minute of Consent to short notice was duly read.
QUORUM	:	The Chairman declared a quorum present and the Meeting duly convened.
DIRECTORS' REPORT AND ACCOUNTS	:	The Directors' Report and Accounts for the period to were duly approved.
AUDITORS	:	It was resolved by Special Resolution that the Company being a dormant company in terms of section 250 of the Companies Act 1985, dispense with the appointment of Auditors.
REMUNERATION OF DIRECTORS	:	It was resolved that no remuneration be paid to the Directors of the Company for the period under review.
DIVIDEND	:	It was resolved on the recommendation of the Directors, that no dividend be paid at this time.

____

Chairman

The Companies Acts 1985 and 1989

Private Company Limited by Shares

SPECIAL RESOLUTION OF LIMITED (NO.)

At the Annual General Meeting of the Members of the above named Company duly convened and held at on the day of Nineteen Hundred and the following Resolution was passed as a SPECIAL RESOLUTION:

THAT the Company, being a dormant company in terms of section 250 of the Companies Act 1985, dispense with the appointment of Auditors.

Certified a true copy

Company Secretaries.

________________________LIMITED

REPORT OF THE DIRECTORS
AND
STATEMENT OF ACCOUNTS

for the period ended

Directors

Secretaries

Banker

Auditors

Registered Office

________________________LIMITED

Report by the Directors
to the
Annual General Meeting of the
Shareholders of
to be held in the Registered Office of the
Company, on

____

The Directors now present the Company's Accounts for the period from   to

The Net Revenue for the year amounted to NIL.

Principal Activity
The business of the Company is

Directors
The Directors of the Company throughout the period and at the date of this Report are as detailed on the first page.

The Directors of the Company holding Shares throughout the period and their respective interests in the Share Capital of the Company were:

	19_	19_
	1 share	1 share
	1 share	1 share

Auditors
In accordance with Section 250 of the Companies Act 1985 a resolution dispensing with the appointment of Auditors will be proposed at the Annual General Meeting.

On behalf of the Board

Company Secretaries

______________________LIMITED

Balance Sheet as at

19__	*Current Assets*	19__
£___	Amount due by Subscribers to Memorandum	£__
	Represented by	
	Share Capital	
	£100 Authorised—100 Shares of £1 each	
£___	Issued and Fully Paid Shares of £1 each	£__

Notes:

During the period from
to the Company did not trade.
We have relied on the exemptions for individual Accounts, on the grounds that the Company is entitled to those exemptions as a small Company, and we certify that the Company was dormant (as defined by Section 250 of the Companies Act 1985) throughout the period from to

Director

SCHEDULE 16

LETTER OF INDEMNITY

DATE:

The Directors,

Limited/PLC,

Dear Sirs,
I hereby make intimation to you that I have lost or mislaid my Share Certificate in respect of Ordinary Shares in your Company. I declare that the said Certificate has not been lodged with any Bank or any other financial institution as security for any loan granted to me and I hereby declare that, should the said Certificate come to light at any time in the future, I shall immediately forward it to you; And I hereby undertake to indemnify your Company against any actions, proceedings, costs, claims, losses or liabilities whatsoever (including reasonable legal fees and expenses) in connection with the loss of the said Certificate.

Dated this day of 19

Note: Under English law a letter in this form should be executed as a deed or else some consideration for the issue of the letter will be required.

SCHEDULE 17

MINUTE OF FIRST BOARD MEETING

MINUTE OF THE FIRST MEETING of the Directors of held at on the day of 19 .

Present:

In Attendance:

Apologies:

1. *Chairman:*

It was agreed that should act as Chairman of the Meeting. The Chairman noted that a quorum was present and declared the Meeting duly convened.

2. *Incorporation:*

It was recorded that the Company had been incorporated on the day of 19 (No.) [and that by [Ordinary and] Special Resolution[s] passed on [and], [the share capital of the Company had been increased to £] [and] [the name of the Company had been changed from Limited to " Limited"], [and] [a new principal objects clause [and new Articles of Association] had been adopted.] The Certificate of Incorporation, [Certificate of Incorporation on Change of Name] and prints of the Company's Memorandum and Articles of Association [as amended/adopted] were produced to the Meeting.

[3.] *Appointment of Directors and Resignation of First Directors:*

It was recorded that the first Directors of the Company who had held office for incorporation purposes had resigned, following the appointment of the present Directors. A written memorandum in that respect dated was tabled. The relevant Forms 288 intimating such appointments and resignations had been filed with the Registrar of Companies and the appropriate entries made in the Company's statutory registers.

[4.] *Secretary*:

A letter of resignation by , the first Secretary of the Company, who had held office for incorporation purposes only, was tabled and accepted and it was resolved that be appointed Secretary in their stead.
intimated acceptance of office and the appropriate Form 288 was signed for filing with the Registrar of Companies. The appropriate entry was made in the Company's statutory registers.

[5.] *Registered office:*

It was noted that the Registered Office of the Company had been fixed on incorporation at
[and it was resolved that the Registered Office be changed to . The appropriate notice to the Registrar of Companies, Form 287, was signed.] The Secretary was instructed to [file same and to] arrange for the appropriate notice to be affixed at the entrance of the Registered Office.

[6.] *Statutory Registers*:

The Statutory Registers of the Company were produced to the Meeting. It was resolved that these be kept by the Secretary at the Registered Office.

[It was resolved that the Statutory Registers of the company be kept by at and the appropriate notice to the Registrar of Companies, Form 353, was signed for filing with the Registrar.]

[7.] *Auditors*:

It was resolved that , Chartered Accountants, be appointed Auditors of the Company in terms of the Companies Act 1985. The Secretary was instructed to write to intimating their appointment and requesting confirmation of their acceptance of office.

[8.] *Accounting Reference Date*:

It was resolved that the Company's accounting Reference Date be in each year. The appropriate Form 225 was signed and the Secretary was directed to file same with the Registrar of Companies.

[9.] *Share Transfers*:

Duly stamped transfers signed by both transferor and transferee of the [two] unpaid subscribers' share(s) were tabled and approved as follows:

Transferor	*Transferee*	*No. of Shares*

It was resolved that these shares be paid up in full in cash immediately and remittances from the shareholders were delivered accordingly. The Secretary was instructed to register the transferees in the Register of Members as holders of said shares.

[10.] *Allotment of Shares*:

The Chairman reported that the undernoted applications for shares had been received, viz:

Applicant	*Number of Shares*	*Class of Shares*

After consideration the applications were approved and it was resolved that in exchange for the relevant remittances such shares be forthwith allotted and issued to the Applicants credited as fully paid. Remittances for the shares having been received, the Secretary was instructed to register the Applicants in the Register of Members as holders of the said Shares and to file the necessary Form[s] [88(2) [and] 88(3)] with the Registrar of Companies.

[11.] *Share Certificates*

Share Certificates made out in favour of the holders of the Shares specified in paragraphs [10 and 11] above were tabled signed by and and delivered to the Shareholders.

[12.] *Banking Requirements*

It was resolved that a banking account or accounts for the Company be opened with and the said Bank is hereby empowered:

(1) To honour and debit to the Company's account or accounts all Cheques, Bills of Exchange, Promissory Notes, Dividend or Interest Warrants or other Orders for payment drawn, accepted or made by on behalf of the Company whether the account or accounts of the Company be overdrawn by the payment thereof or otherwise.

(2) To treat all Bills and Promissory Notes as duly drawn or endorsed on behalf of the Company and to discount or otherwise deal with the same, provided they are signed by [*e.g.* any two directors].

(3) To treat all Cheques, Bills of Exchange, Promissory Notes, Drafts and Orders as duly endorsed on behalf of the Company when signed by [*e.g.* any two directors].

(4) To pay on the endorsement of any Deposit Receipts which the Company may have from time to time.

(5) To deliver on the order of any securities which may from time to time be pledged to or lodged with the Bank by or on behalf of the Company.

[13.] *Statutory Requirements*:

The attention of the Directors was drawn to:

(1) Sections 348, 349, 350 and 351 of the Companies Act 1985 which provide that every Company must:
  (a) display a notice specifying its full registered name at its principal places of business;
  (b) state its full registered name in all business letters, notices, official publications, invoices, bills, cheques, receipts, etc;
  (c) state its country of registration, its Registered Number and the address of its Registered Office in all business letters and order forms.

(2) Section 305 of the Companies Act 1985 which provides that although there is no requirement to state names of Directors on business papers of the Company, if Directors' names are stated, then the full names (or initials and surnames) of all the Directors of the Company must be stated.

(3) Sections 324, 325 and 326 of the Companies Act 1985 which provide that all Directors of the Company must notify the Company in writing of all interests of themselves, their spouses and children in the Share Capital or Debentures of the Company and must notify the Company of these interests and changes in same within five days of becoming aware of the same.

(4) Section 4 of the Business Names Act 1985 which provides that every Company which carries on business under a name other than its full registered name must:
 (a) display in any premises where the business is carried on a notice specifying the Company's full registered name and an address at which service of any document relating to the business may be effected;
 (b) specify the Company's full registered name and an address at which service of any document relating to the business may be effected in all business letters, written orders, invoices, receipts, etc. of the business.

[14.] *Closure of Meeting*

The business of the Meeting having been concluded the Chairman declared the Meeting closed.

....
Chairman

SCHEDULE 18

MINUTE OF ANNUAL GENERAL MEETING

______________________LIMITED

MINUTE OF THE
ANNUAL GENERAL MEETING of the above named
Company held at
on the day of
19

Present: (Chairman)

In Attendance:

Notice: The Notice calling the Meeting [including Minute of consent to short Notice] was duly read.

Quorum: The Chairman declared a quorum present and the Meeting duly convened.

Minutes of Last AGM: The Minutes of the last Annual General Meeting were read and approved.

Auditors' Report: The Auditors' Report was read.

Directors' Report and Accounts: The Directors' Report and Accounts for the [year to] [period from to] were approved.

Appointment of Auditors: It was resolved that be appointed Auditors, to hold office from the conclusion of this Meeting until the conclusion of the next Annual General Meeting. The directors are authorised to settle the remuneration of the Auditors.

Directors' Remuneration: (a) It was resolved that no remuneration be paid to the Directors for the year under review.

(b) It was resolved that remuneration for the following Directors be paid as follows:

Election of Directors: (a) In accordance with the Articles of Association of the Company
retire(s) from office by rotation and, being eligible was/were duly re-elected as (a) Director(s).

(b) No Director retires from office by rotation at this time.

(c) In accordance with the Articles of Association of the Company
having been appointed [as an additional director] [to fill a vacancy as director] by the directors subsequent to the last annual general meeting [stood down from office] [offered himself/herself for re-election and was duly re-elected as a director]

Declaration of Dividend: (a) The Board resolved not to pay a dividend at this time.

(b) The Board having resolved to pay a dividend of do not recommend any further payments for the year to

Closure of Meeting: The business of the meeting having been concluded the Chairman declared the meeting closed.

____

Chairman

SCHEDULE 19

USEFUL ADDRESSES

The Registrar of Companies
(England and Wales)
Companies House
Crown Way
Maindy
Cardiff CF4 3UZ
Tel: 01222 388588

The Registrar of Companies
(Scotland)
Argylle House
37 Castle Terrace
Edinburgh EH1 2EB
Tel: 0131 535 5800
or 55-71 City Road
London EC1Y 1BB
Tel: 0171 253 9393

H.M. Customs and Excise
New King's Beam House
22 Upper Ground,
London SE1 9PJ
Tel: 0171 620 1313

Inland Revenue Stamp Office
Bush House, Strand
South West Wing
London WC2B 4QN
Tel: 0171 438 6622

Controller of Stamps
Mulberry House
16 Picardy Place
Edinburgh EH1 3NF
Tel: 0131 556 8998

The Institute of Directors
116 Pall Mall, London SW1Y 5ED
Tel: 0171 839 1233

Panel on Take-Overs and Mergers
PO Box 226
20th Floor
The Stock Exchange Building
London EC2P 2JX
Tel: 0171 382 9026

The London Stock Exchange
Old Broad Street
London EC2N 1HP
Tel: 0171 588 2355

The Aim Team
London Stock Exchange
Old Broad Street
London EC2N 1HP
Tel: 0171 797 4404

Crest Co. Publications
Trinity Tower
9 Thomas More Street
London E1 9YN
Tel: 0171 459 3001

INDEX